SEA AND RIVER PILOTS

Other books by Nancy Martin — A selection

Non Fiction

    The Post Office—From Carrier Pigeon to Confravision (Dents).
    The Fire Service Today (Dents).
    Search and Rescue—The Story of the Coastguard Service (David & Charles).

School Books

    Finn the Fisherboy (Macmillan).
    Three Horses (Macmillan).
    Three Dogs (Macmillan).
    Three at the Zoo (Macmillan).

Career Books

    Teresa Joins the Red Cross (Macmillan).
    Call the Nurse (Macmillan).
    Four Girls in a Store (Macmillan).

Biography

    William Carey—The Man Who Never Gave Up (Hodder & Stoughton).

Anthology

    Prayers for Children and Young People (Hodder & Stoughton).

SEA AND RIVER PILOTS

by

NANCY MARTIN

TERENCE DALTON LIMITED
LAVENHAM . SUFFOLK
1977

Published by
TERENCE DALTON LIMITED
ISBN 0 900963 72 7

Set in 10/12pt English

Printed in Great Britain at
THE LAVENHAM PRESS LIMITED
LAVENHAM   .   SUFFOLK

Contents

Index of Illustrations

Trinity House Pilot boat *St Clement* at 25 knots off the Needles.

Halmatic Limited

Acknowledgements

This book could not have been written but for the courtesy and co-operation of Mr R. S. Soames, Trinity House Pilotage Department; Mr E. Eden, General Secretary and Legal Adviser of the United Kingdom Pilots' Association (also Secretary-General of the International Maritime Pilots' Association), and Miss Yvonne Blake, Assistant to Mr Eden. Besides answering innumerable questions and providing much printed and photographic material, they arranged for me to visit pilot stations and meet pilots at fifteen ports in the United Kingdom.

Mr A. de Vries, President of the European Maritime Pilots' Association, was equally helpful and informative during the time I was in Rotterdam and Europort, personally conducting me on visits to pilots on station and arranging with Shell Tankers (UK) for me to inspect the 278,220 ton oil tanker *Latirus* after she had discharged her cargo at Europort.

To all these officials and to the many pilots around the coast who gave so freely of their time and experience, enabling me to see them at work, I gratefully acknowledge my indebtedness.

I also wish to thank the many authorities and individuals who have loaned photographs for reproduction in the book and which are duly acknowledged.

My thanks are also expressed to Phyllis Lovelock for checking and clerical assistance.

Nancy Martin
Fittleworth, Sussex

February 1977

Oil tanker ss *Latia.*

Introduction

"PILOTS are trustworthiness personified," wrote Joseph Conrad, who, before becoming an author at the turn of the century, was master of a merchant ship.

It has also been said that "a pilot needs to know almost everything without having to consult anything."

These comments are certainly true of the men navigating today's shipping, with its enormous cargoes carried in vessels ranging from coasters and cargo boats, to trawlers, container ships and oil tankers. A container ship may be three times the length of a football pitch, and stand forty feet above the quay when unloaded, while a 250,000 ton crude oil carrier (V.L.C.C.)* is equal in length and as much as forty-five feet above its berth after discharging its oil. Navigating such vessels through narrow channels, knowing the exact position of sandbanks, the nature and whereabouts of shifting shoals, rocks and other hazards of the sea bed, depths of water and position of navigating aids, is only part of a pilot's duty. He has to be fully conversant with the sophisticated equipment on the bridge and give clear and confident orders to those concerned with steering the ship in terms which they will understand. He has his charts, though he is so familiar with the area he seldom has to consult them. The buoys in the river Humber are moved forty-five to sixty times a year owing to the fresh water and mud in the river, which could be most confusing to a master or mate unfamiliar with the fact, but pilots are kept informed of any such movements. It is also part of their duty to observe these things and report them to the right authorities.

There must be few people who are unaware of the great work done by those who man the lifeboats around the coasts. The same might be said of lighthouse keepers, coastguards and those who serve on lightships; yet the 15,000 sea and river pilots throughout the world who render equally important service to the seagoing community are largely unrecognised.

In general the public only begins to realise what is involved in pilotage when newspapers carry headlines such as:

"Pilot Dies as Gales Hit Coast! Captain Laurence Mitchell, Senior Trinity House Pilot at Falmouth, fell to his death, on 2nd September 1974 while trying to board a shipping casualty, the car ferry Eagle, in Falmouth Bay last night, a victim of the storm force winds which swept the West Country."

Further enlightenment of the responsibilities and risks run by pilots was provided in the television programme in which some Trinity House pilots drew attention to the hazards of piloting super oil tankers through congested waters.

Those who travel on passenger ships are often sufficiently curious to watch the pilot board the vessel to bring it into port. They will pass the word around—"The pilot has come aboard,"—and may experience a greater feeling of security, but there interest will end. Only when incidents receive banner headlines does the public in general realise something of the hazards to which pilots are continually exposed; yet the effects of bad pilotage

*Very Large Crude Carrier.

A Buoy-tender replacing a light-buoy at sea.   *Royal Netherlands Navy*

include loss of life, injury to persons and property, wrecks and consequent blocking of ports, sometimes with resultant dangers of explosions and pollution.

One London river pilot remarked: "Anybody who says he knows all about this river (The Thames) is either a genius or a fool. I have been here forty-two years and I have not met a genius yet."

A pilot has to think ahead yet go on board with a completely open mind—ready to make quick adjustments to any plans he has regarding the handling of the vessel. The wind may be different, the tide and the ship different—even if the ship is known to him it is still different from previous occasions on which he has handled it. One pilot confessed that, although he had served for ten years as an apprentice, he was terrified when he took a ship out for the first time. Now, after piloting for very many years he says once he steps on board a ship he gets the feel of it and if he feels satisfied it doesn't matter if there is dense fog, or if it is blowing a gale, he knows he can cope. Yet he is always aware of what could happen with a big vessel swinging into a jetty or coming off. What happens, for instance, if the towline parts?

When a pilot boards a ship in his official capacity he is wholly and solely responsible for piloting it. No one can release him from that responsibility and no one, except the master of the ship, is permitted to interfere with his conduct of the pilotage. The master remains in administrative and executive control but gives the charge of navigation to the pilot and very rarely interferes.

Climbing-up the pilot ladder.   *Royal Netherlands Navy*

The Steering Committee on Pilotage, in their Report to the Secretary of State in June 1974, summarised the situation as follows:

"The master retains the supreme authority on board and may, where essential for safety, override the pilot."

The Report added, however, "On balance, we recommend against attempting to spell out this relationship in a new Act. We also recommend that the provisions of the 1913 Act regarding the pilot's responsibility to the shipowner should be left unchanged."

The Section of the Act referred to (Section 15) clearly states that "when a vessel is under such pilotage the owner or master is answerable for any loss or damage caused by the vessel just as if pilotage were not compulsory."

But the pilot does not escape his responsibilities. If damage occurs to any ship in the charge of a pilot, he must make a full written report to the pilotage authority from which he holds his licence. Should the case be a serious one he will be required to appear before a meeting of the Authority or its pilotage committee to explain matters and justify his conduct of the pilotage operation; failure to do so could have serious consequences. He may be censured, have his licence suspended for a period, or revoked, though, in the latter two cases, he has a right of appeal to the Civil Courts.

Pilotage is a co-operative function in which a number of men are involved; masters and crews of ships, tug operators, boatmen, shore mooring parties, harbour masters and docking masters. Upon their ability to perform their duties properly may depend the pilot's reputation. He is the leader of a team not of his own choosing or his own training, although most are reasonably skilled, experienced men, responsible in their own right for their own actions, yet fully appreciative of the responsibility borne by the pilot.

In addition to ensuring the safe passage and berthing of a ship one of the most important duties of a pilot today is to expedite its passage. With their vast experience pilots are able to bring ships in and out of a port more quickly than anyone else; they know that losing a tide can make a difference of ten to twelve hours. Even a 1,000-ton coaster can lose £450 a day, while a mere hour's delay with a tanker could cost the owners £1,000. Pilots boast that they can handle the largest ships and put them alongside a quay in such a manner that they would not crack an egg. A ship must be in the right place, at the right time, at the right speed, and it is the pilot's task to see that this happens when handling a vessel. Efficient pilotage can do much to reduce costs and improve the turn around of traffic in a port.

The purpose of this book is to show how the pilotage service functions in different parts of the world in order to achieve this.

Pilots plotting course.

CHAPTER ONE

Early History

THE earliest name by which pilots were known was *Lodesman,* or *Lotesman* in German, a term which has the same root as the *Lodestone*, a piece of magnetic ore which had the effect of turning in a north or south direction when suspended. It was used as a compass, or direction finder.

The term *pilot* originated from the Dutch words *Pijl*, meaning anything vertically straight, and *Leod*, a lead which is sent down in a straight line to determine the depth of water at a given point.

Another term used was *Hovellers*, which is the name still applied to the men who board barges to work them under bridges.

Since earliest times demands have been made that ships nearing or leaving the confined waters of a harbour should be conducted by experienced men who are aware of the problems of navigation within their own locality. From small beginnings many years ago, pilotage has become an indispensable part of navigation. It is international in concept and action, and while each country has its own laws and regulations, in the main differences of operation are minimal. The objective is the same all over the world—the safe conduct of ships through a river, road or channel, from or into a port. A pilot is a person taken on board at a particular place to do just that.

The increase in trade and industry over the centuries, resulting in greater and more varied cargoes, bigger and better ports, larger and more advanced types of ships, has created its own problems, with pilots becoming more and more essential.

Pilotage is of ancient origin, though it has to be remembered that, at one time, officers who had charge of the helm of a ship on which they were serving, were also known as pilots. As long ago as 1700 B.C. Hammurabi's Babylonian Code of Laws included statutes relating to pilots' fees being two shekels of silver, the seafarers' silver. Also included in these laws were penalties for accidents and the loss of ships.

There are references to pilots in the Bible. For example, Ezekiel, who is thought to have lived approximately six centuries before Christ, had the following to say:

"Thy wise men, O Tyrus, that were in thee were thy pilots. The suburbs shall shake at the sound of the cry of thy pilots, and all that handle the oar, the mariners and all the pilots of the sea, shall come down from their ships."*

Another mention of pilots is in the Rhodian Law, operating early in the third century when Rhodes was a famous Greek island holding sovereignty of the Aegean Sea, with well-built ships "splendidly manned and manoeuvred." Article II states: "the wages of the pilot shall be a portion and a half," which some think may mean that pilots received one and a half times that of a regular seaman.

Ezekiel, Chapter 27, verses 8, 28, 29.

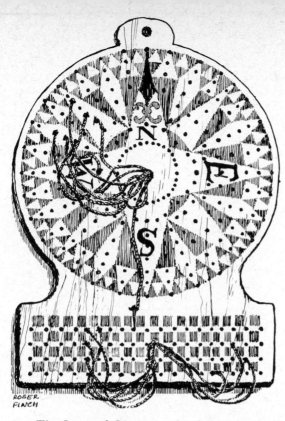

Wooden traverse board, an early navigation instrument dating from early 16th century.
Drawing by Roger Finch from his "Coals from Newcastle"

The Laws of Oleron, a tiny island in the Bay of Biscay, are still the basis of modern maritime law. They were intended for the use of mariners in Atlantic waters and were introduced into England in the twelfth century, and into Flanders in the thirteenth. Drastic penalties were laid down for losing a ship; a pilot who lost his ship by default was to be "taken to the windlass and there beheaded by the crew, and the crew were not to be answerable to any judge because the *Lodesman* had committed high treason against his undertaking of pilotage."

When the Laws were introduced into England the pilot's penalty for losing a ship was that he be hanged at the yard-arm; a law which was passed in the hope that it might act as a deterrent to the purposeful wrecking of ships for the benefit of the salvage obtainable. Plundering was legal if no living creature came ashore and some boatmen and fishermen who served as pilots were unscrupulous.

Another Oleron Law enacted that when two wine ships collided damages were to be divided equally between the owners, regardless of the party responsible for the accident. There was an interesting sequel to this when a service was held in St Paul's Cathedral to commemorate the sixth century of the Court of Admiralty, and the eighth of the promulgation of the Laws of Oleron by Eleanor of Aquitaine, in 1160. It was a ceremonial occasion, with a copy of the Laws of Oleron being officially handed over to the Chaplain of the Fleet with these words:

"We ask you to accept this copy of the Laws and cause it to be conveyed in one of Her Majesty's ships with our greetings to the islanders of Oleron."

In his sermon Dr Fisher, then Archibishop of Canterbury, referred to the law framed to put an end to the dishonest practice of skippers of old ships deliberately colliding with others in order to claim damages.

Many travellers and explorers employed pilots. Marco Polo took Arab pilots and when he was delayed at points in Southern India on his return journey to Venice, in 1292, he spent a considerable time studying sea charts with them.

In 1498, Arab pilots were actively engaged in navigation in the Near East and in the Indian Ocean. Vasco da Gama employed such pilots on his first journey around the Cape of Good Hope en route to India. Juan de la Costa, with his square rigged vessel *Santa Maria*, was chief pilot to Columbus on the first of his two expeditions to the New World, although in this case the term "pilot" may well have been used in the sense of master of the craft.

The defeat of the Spanish ships in the Armada has been attributed, in part, to the fact that they were unable to reach Dunkirk, where they intended to take on pilots and charts.

John Cabot, who had settled in Bristol as a merchant, set sail from that port in 1497 on a voyage of discovery. He took with him his three sons, one of whom, Sebastian, was later appointed by Henry VIII as Grand Pilot of England; the Spanish king, Charles V, made him Pilot Major of Spain. George Ray, one of the first Bristol pilots, formerly a barge master, accompanied the expedition in his capacity as pilot.

These voyages of discovery were the prelude to important changes in English commerce, shipping and navigation. As overseas trade increased, and navigational aids improved, new sea routes were opened and experienced pilots were needed. Until the fifteenth century pilots were not expected to have detailed knowledge of the ports to which they were guiding the ship; they were only required to know the location and general shape of the coastline, possibly from their experience as former masters of ships, but as ships became larger, local pilots were employed.

For years London enjoyed the greater part of trade, with the main shipping route London to Antwerp. With the operation of the new sea routes, and the difficulty of bringing large sailing ships into and out of the Thames, London began to lose this preponderance. Southampton became popular as an outport of London. Ports such as Exeter, Hull, Newcastle and Plymouth were successfully operating; Hull and Newcastle having their own Trinity Houses controlling pilotage.

Despite the increase in trade the British merchant fleet compared unfavourably with European. Even at the beginning of Elizabeth's reign the British merchant fleet consisted of no more than 1,600 ships, only 250 of which were over 80 tons. Development in ship design and navigational aids came very slowly. While the properties of the compass had been known by European mariners from the twelfth century, navigators had no means of finding their longitude when out of sight of land, their ability to navigate depending on the use they could make of landmarks, such as churches and prominent buildings, and their knowledge of tides and sandbanks. With no charts to assist them they made sketches of the coastline, harbours and rivers, making allowances as best they could for tide and current and bad steering, and trying not to lose sight of land.

Masters sailing up the Thames were warned not to "lose sight of the spyre of the steeple of Margat behind the land, for then you should come too neere it. But if you keepe so far from the shore, that you can see that foresaid steeple above the high land, or keep it even in your sight, then you cannot take hurt of the South grounds."

That such seamarks were needed was shown in a report which reads:

"And many sands, shallows and flatts reach many miles into the maine sea, lying from thence dispersed up to the estuarie or fote of the Thames, commonly changing the usuall channell . . . pilots dare not adventure to crosse or come nigh to them without conduct of beacons."

Beacons, as then known, were poles set in the seabed or on the shore, often with a lantern fixed on top.

John Harrison's chronometer was not invented and built until 1735, while communications, if they existed at all, were of the most primitive; pilots had to sit in their boats watching and waiting for the arrival of vessels which might need them. There were few, if any, buoys even in such dangerous channels as the Thames Estuary, Dungeness and the Goodwins; those which did exist were of the simplest, being described as "square pieces of timber six or eight feet fastened to a chayne of iron." Lighthouses and other seamarks were almost non-existent.

Navigation in the lower reaches of the Thames presented its own problems. Manoeuvring of the square riggers in use at that time, coupled with the direction of prevailing winds, was difficult and dangerous. The silting of the river was another hazard, and this was not really dealt with until the middle of the seventeenth century. An Armada pilot declared:

"From the Cape at North Foreland to the river at Rochester, where the Queen's fleet lies, and then on to London, it is necessary to take on pilots from the same country, since the shoals are shifting."

From the middle of the fifteenth century the Hanseatic League insisted on the

Donna Nook Beacon, Lower Humber, 1835.   Brough Beacon, Upper Humber, 1863.

Trinity House, Kingston-upon-Hull

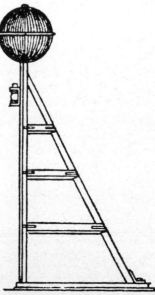

employment of local pilots when entering and leaving harbours. There was an urgent need for Britain to regulate pilotage in the Thames, where younger men, lacking in knowledge and experience, were proving unsuitable as pilots and putting ships and people at risk. Not only were these so-called pilots pushing out older and more experienced men, but they were only prepared to negotiate the Thames. They had no knowledge of seamanship and did not attempt to acquire it.

With a limited number of trained seamen, the time was ripe for an organised pilotage service. Trinity House, London, was already in existence as an Association of Shipmen and Mariners of a semi-religious character, with benevolent objects. Now they petitioned for a charter from Henry VIII. The petition read:

"Wherfortyme owte of mynde as long as due order good rule and guydyng were suffird to be had in your said Ryver and other places by aunctent English maisters and lodesmen of the same, the said rivers and places and the daungers of the same were then by theym thrughly serchid so surely that fewe shippes or noon were perished in defaulte of lodemanage. Now it is so moste gracious sovereign lord, that dyvers and many youngmen namyng theymself maryners beyng owte of all good order and rule, not havyng the perfyte knowlege ne experience in shipmen's crafte, neither of sufficiency experience approved ne of age in the same to know the suraunce and saufconduyte of shippes by the comyng of lodemanage, dailly vnseytly medle therewith to greate hurte and losse of moche of the said Navye."

The king was fully occupied with the war with France and the Charter was not granted until 20th May, 1514, when it gave official recognition to Trinity House and general powers for the safety and progress of shipping. By-laws were passed giving the Corporation effective control of pilotage in the Thames. Ninety years later James I granted Trinity House the compulsory pilotage of shipping and the exclusive right to licence pilots in the River. With good reason the men appointed had to be bold and fearless.

In 1561 an Act was passed giving the Corporation powers to erect "beacons, marks and signs of the sea . . . whereby the dangers may be avoided and escaped and ships the better come unto their ports without peril."

The Corporation was given the general oversight of seamarks throughout England and, by an Act passed in 1594, the beaconage and buoyage of the Thames was made their specific charge.

Six years after the first charter had been granted there were forty licensed London river pilots. In that time they had not lost a ship; they were all self-employed, a situation which has continued to the present day. Samuel Pepys, who had done much to improve the Navy, was appointed First Master in 1685.

Two other seamen's organisations were granted charters by Henry VIII. Trinity House of Newcastle, formed in 1536, was given powers to regulate pilotage in the Tyne. Trinity House of Kingston-upon-Hull, a Guild or Fraternity of Masters and Pilots, founded in 1369, was granted its charter in 1541. Pilotage on the Humber River had been in operation from 1512. The Masters of Hulks, whose infrequent voyages to the river had given them insufficient experience in navigating there, asked Trinity House "to assign to

Cinque Port Warrant, 1739.

Trinity House, London

To all to whom these Presents shall come, WHEREAS by an Act of Parliament made in the Fifth Year of the Reign of His Majesty King GEORGE the Second, intituled, *An Act for the better Regulation and Government of Pilots, licensed by the Corporation of Trinity-House of Deptford-Strond, in the County of* Kent, *and to prevent Mischiefs and Annoyances upon the River of* Thames *below* London-Bridge. It is amongst other Things enacted, That from and after the Twenty-fourth Day of *June*, One Thousand Seven Hundred and Thirty Two, If any Person shall take upon himself the Charge of any Ship or Vessel, as Pilot, down the River of *Thames*, or through the North Channel to or by *Orfordness*, or round the Long-Sand-Head into the *Downs*, or down the South Channel into the *Downs*, or from or by *Orfordness* up the North Channel, or the River of *Thames*, or the River *Medway*, other than such Person as shall be licensed and authorized to Act as Pilot, by the Master, Wardens and Assistants of the Corporation of *Trinity-House* of *Deptford-Strond*, in the County of *Kent*, under the Common Seal of the said Corporation, then such Person shall, for every such Offence, forfeit the Sum of Twenty Pounds. And whereas by long Usage, and by divers Charters and Grants from the Crown, as well as by the said Act of Parliament, the said Corporation are impowered to License and Authorize all Pilots for the conducting Ships and Vessels within the Limits aforesaid : Now KNOW YE, That we the said Master, Wardens and Assistants, do hereby certify and declare, That we have Examined the Bearer hereof *Mr Francis Brooke of Margate*

Mariner, and do find and judge him to be an able and fit Person to be intrusted with the Piloting of Ships and Vessels. *from London down the River of Thames to the South Channel into the Downes*

And We do therefore License, Authorize, and Impower Him the said *Francis Brooke*

to Act as a Pilot accordingly, so long as he shall be found capable of well executing the said Office of a Pilot, and conform himself to the Regulation and Government of the said Corporation, and shall particularly observe the Rules and Orders hereunto annex'd, and such other Rules and Orders as he shall from Time to Time receive in Writing from the said Corporation, for the publick Service, agreeable to the Tenour and Intent of the said Act of Parliament and Charters. In TESTIMONY whereof We have caused the Common Seal of the Corporation to be hereunto affixed, this *fourth* Day of *July* 1759.

them good men and able to bring in their ships called Hulks into the port of Hull. And they would be glad to pay for bringing in of every one of their said ships six shillings and eight pence and for the bringing forth of the ships out of the river called Humber, twenty shillings sterling money."

The difference in payment for the inward and outward journey was doubtless accounted for by the difference in place at which pilots would board the ship on the two journeys. Here, as elsewhere, there were no navigational aids or seamarks to guide ships away from the treacherous sandbanks.

Pilotage was originally organised on a voluntary basis, but when the king saw a stranger bringing his ship into Hull without a pilot, he decreed:

"Whensoever any ship or ships being Foreign or Foreigners, as Frenchmen, Dutchmen, Scots or Easterlings or any other Foreigner of outward Realm or Realms whatsoever that shall come to the said Town, they must employ one of the Masters of the House to bring the ship in."

Such pilots were to be paid:

2s. 4d. for every ship of 20 tons and under
3s. 4d. for every ship above 20 tons and under 40 tons
5s. 0d. for those of 40 tons to 60 tons
and 6s. 8d. for those of 60 tons to 100 tons and above.

Queen Elizabeth's charter of 1581 extended the Guild's powers as a pilotage authority and four years later it was given the right to make a charge on cargo passing in and out of Hull by sea.

Possession of a charter did not mean that its provisions commanded automatic obedience. Some seamen refused to pay their dues but the Brethren of Trinity House were zealous in the enforcement of their powers, and the High Court issued a warrant for the arrest of defaulting masters and pilots.

Equally, men acting as pilots who were not appointed by Trinity House, were fined. One such was fined forty shillings "provided it be paid this night, otherwise £3. 6s. 8d."

Yet the practice continued, with unskilled men constantly piloting ships into danger, while the Brethren sought to impose their authority by all the means within their power.

"In 1705 William Simpson, having piloted a vessel without the Warden's order, was condemned in twenty shillings forfeiture."

"In 1766 Christopher Dresser a Young Brother having put his son on board a ship to pilot her up the Humber, who ran the said ship ashore, was disfranchised, mulched of his Pilotage and deprived of his weekly allowance from the House."

"In 1767, Complaint having been made that Robert Dale had ran a vessel whereof he was Pilot ashore in Humber and he attending the Board according to direction, but giving no satisfactory reason for making that mistake was ordered to deliver up his Branch* and not to take charge for the future until he produced a testimonial on his better qualifications and of his sobriety."

Such unsatisfactory pilotage not only caused loss of life and injury to people or property, but the ports were blocked by wrecks.

*A Branch is a pilot's certificate.

Humber pilots appointed by the Brethren of Trinity House of Kingston-upon-Hull were already subject to a detailed and demanding examination, and merchants and ship owners, as well as Trinity House, were most concerned by the operations of unskilled men who undertook pilotage duties. As a result, the Brethren made successful application for an Act to be passed to prevent illegal piloting and to make pilotage of the Humber compulsory.

The Act passed by Parliament in 1800 greatly increased the powers of Trinity House, Kingston-upon-Hull, who were appointed the pilotage authority whose duty it was to examine and licence pilots, fine unauthorised pilots, suspend and, where necessary, cancel pilot licences. The only exemptions from compulsory pilotage were men of war, coasters, British vessels of less than six feet draught and vessels coming into the Humber for shelter. A charge of not more than six guineas was imposed on pilots for their initial licence and not more than three guineas for their annual renewal. The Act also fixed pilotage rates for British ships. Less than a month after the Act was passed thirty mariners were granted licences and such certificates, which contained the seal of Trinity House Corporation, had to be carried and shown on demand to masters of vessels.

Although, in 1585, authority was granted to the Pilotage Authority to place buoys and beacons for the better conducting, guiding, safeguarding and passing of ships in and out of the River Humber, this was carried out so slowly that thirty years later there were only two beacons and one unlit buoy. All pilotage in the river had to be performed during daylight because of this lack of seamarks; vessels having to drop anchor at night and wait for daybreak.

Hull pilots, 1898.

Liverpool Pilot boats. Left the 62 ton schooner *The Duke* and right the 61 ton *Queen* built at Cowes in 1856.

J. Delacour-Keir

By the time of the national census in 1801, Hull had become the fourth port in the country, with a population of nearly 30,000 as against only 6,000 to 7,000 a century earlier. The three ports which handled a larger volume of trade were London, Liverpool and Bristol. Trade was still increasing in Hull and a new dock was opened to accommodate the greater number of ships using the port, while the number of pilots increased from thirty to forty-one. All were well trained but the change of ship propulsion from sail to steam created a new technique for them to master. The change took place over a considerable period of time and there were still a few sailing vessels operating as late as the end of the nineteenth century.

The Liverpool Pilot Service was not officially established until 1766, with the passing of an Act appointing as Commissioners the "Mayor, Aldermen, Bailiffs and Common Council men of the Borough and Corporation, together with Merchants, Mariners and late Commanders of Vessels."

There is little doubt that a system of pilotage was in existence long before that date, probably with fishermen acting as pilots, but the need for an established system became apparent in 1764 when 18 ships were stranded, with the loss of 75 lives. Those who framed the Act must have had this in mind when they stated: "The entrance to the port of Liverpool is very dangerous without a skilful pilot, and many ships and lives have, of late years, been lost owing to the negligence and ignorance of persons taking upon them to conduct ships and vessels into and out of the said port."

The Liverpool pilotage district covers a very large area, comprising more than 2,500 square miles of the Irish Sea, bounded by the coasts of Cheshire, Anglesey and Wales, the east side of the Isle of Man, Lancashire and Cumberland as far as St Bees Head. In 1858 Mersey Docks and Harbour Board was properly constituted as the Liverpool Pilotage Authority, but pilots continued to own their boats until 1886 when they were taken over by the Pilotage Authority, although, as in most ports in the United Kingdom, pilots kept their self-employed status.

The early history of Bristol Channel pilotage is rather obscure, but it appears to date back to 1611, when control of most of the Channel was vested in the Society of Merchant Venturers in that city. A number of the smaller Channel ports developed their own system of unlicensed pilots. Cardiff and some other parts tried many times to have the right to appoint their own licensed pilots, but did not succeed in this until 1860, when the number of foreign vessels entering Cardiff was 4,434, compared with only 984 entering Bristol.

Exe Estuary pilots were subject to the authority of Exeter City Chamber in 1687, when pilotage was compulsory for all vessels drawing more than five feet of water, but many authorities warned all masters not to "venture into that place without a pilot." The difficulties of crossing Exmouth Bar and negotiating the shoals in the narrow channels resulted in high pilotage charges which, in 1884, were stated to be among the heaviest in the kingdom. This partly accounted for the decline of the Exe ports in the nineteenth century. Complaints were made by local merchants about these high costs and also concerning the inefficiency of the Exmouth pilots who were also known to be engaged in smuggling activities, so prevalent at that time.

Since then pilotage has reached a high degree of honour and efficiency in practically every part of the world.

Trinity House, London.

Trinity House, London

CHAPTER TWO

Early History — International

BRITAIN is by no means the only country with a long history of pilotage, nor were British pilots confined to serving ships in and around their own coasts.

American pilotage dates from 1694, when the Governor of the colony of New York authorised the issue of the first Sandy Hook pilot licence. Little is known about the early pilots, though from the outset, fierce competition existed, with pilot craft making a mad race to sea to enable their pilots to be the first to reach the incoming vessel and guide her into port. Many pilots, such as those at Sandy Hook, were licensed but had neither the experience nor the skill to act efficiently, their main interest being in the financial returns.

The first Boston lighthouse keeper was a pilot. He was appointed in 1716 but soon found competition too great and successfully petitioned for an established pilot of Boston Harbour. Two boats were then kept in the harbour, identifiable and distinguishable as pilot craft. If other pilots competed to take ships they had to pay half their fees to the Boston Harbour pilots.

Towards the end of the eighteenth century, the first Congress of the United States recognised the occupation of pilotage and legislated to give control to the respective states. New York Sandy Hook pilots are said to have been fair weather men. They cruised around the harbour when the days were fine and the sea reasonably calm, but when bad weather came, and they were most needed, they retired to the tap rooms to play cards, refusing to answer any distress calls until the weather improved.

By 1860 there were 17 pilot boats operating from New York, manned by 42 pilots. New Jersey had four boats and 30 pilots. Locally knowledgeable pilots had been working from San Francisco for twenty-three years before the Mexican Governor appointed Captain W. A. Richardson, Captain of the Port. The following year, 1838, a Federal regulation required all sea-going coast-wise vessels, as well as foreign-going vessels to take pilots, though there were specific exemptions to this regulation. With the gold rush in 1849 a dozen or so unregulated pilots competed to bring ships across the Great Bar to San Francisco Bay. At that time anyone could become a Bar Pilot by declaring himself one, but a year later an Act was passed to enable the Board of Pilot Commissioners to appoint qualified pilots for San Francisco Bar Harbour and San Pablo and Suisan Bays.

Canadian Government pilot regulations have existed since Colonial days, New Brunswick enacting laws as early as 1789, more than half a century before British legislation. More generally the system may be said to date back to 1873, when certain districts were established by the Canadian Parliament. The Governor in Council was empowered to set up other pilotage districts and make the payment of pilotage dues compulsory or non-compulsory in different ports. These provisions were incorporated in the Canadian Shipping Act when it was introduced in 1906.

Australian pilotage authority is vested in the different states, each of which has its own historical background. The Maritime Services Board for New South Wales controls the service from Port Jackson. Whether any pilotage service existed immediately following the arrival of the *First Fleet* is uncertain, but pilots had been operating in a private capacity for three years prior to that date. Collins' Account of the English Colony in May 1702 refers to a fishery being established under a man named Barton, who had formerly been a pilot, and who was to board all ships coming into the harbour and pilot them to the settlement. The first known official mention of a pilot comes much later with reference to Mr William Bowen, in the *Sydney Gazette* of 29th May 1803. There are references to succeeding pilots, one being dismissed after conviction for stealing and embezzlement.

An article in the *Port of Sydney Journal* of July, 1948, by Captain P. Lusher, a first class pilot in Port Jackson, provides the following information of pilotage in that period:

"Rates of pilotage were first gazetted on 18th September, 1813, the charges being, under seven feet draught £4, thence progressively to twenty feet draught £14 and over this £15. Ships not having British or East India Company registry were charged one quarter more. These fees covered the pilot being aboard for up to three complete days, but after that he could charge eight shillings per day detention money. Compulsory pilotage was enacted in the Year 1833 and several pilots were licensed. It seems probable that in this year the issue of licences to pilots and exemption certificates to certain masters commenced. Each pilot provided his own whaleboat and crew and they were in competition with one another.

"That a very indifferent lookout was kept at night in these times is evident. The ship *Edward Lombe* was wrecked on Middle Head in August 1834. Twelve lives were lost and there were seventeen survivors. They were not seen until after daybreak. As a result of this disaster the first light vessel was moored off the north-western corner of the Sow and Pigs shoal in August 1836."

Boston Light Station—America's oldest and most famous light-house. Since 14th September 1716 it has been the scene of storms, shipwrecks and heroic rescues.

U.S. Coastguard History

Many changes in rates took place during the years which followed until, in July 1864, the entire pilotage system was scrapped in favour of competition amongst Sea Pilots. Under this system, in 1875, the total amount received by five pilots was £6,255, the lowest paid of the five receiving £1,016 and the highest £1,434. From these amounts the boat crews had to be paid, although the Government contributed something towards this.

It seems evident that, although pilots were supposed to work in competition with each other, they made their own private arrangements to do the work in turn.

The first pilotage duty in Port Phillip is reputed to have been performed by George Tobin, though pilots had then been operating in a private capacity for three years.

George Tobin was thought to have come from Van Diemen's Land. He applied for a pilot's licence in March 1839, when he was recommended as a "seaman and shipmaster for nearly twenty years who had gained an intimate knowledge of all the channels, soundings, etc., in the bay as well as in the Yarra Yarra River, and as one who had sailed as a master in the West Indian trade."

He was thirty-two years of age and was described as a "sober, steady and industrious man well qualified and fully competent in every respect to hold the situation of pilot."

Others were soon appointed, including one, Trundle, in 1841, though his service appears to have ended when he boarded the *Georgina* "in a tipsy condition and abused the captain and the harbour master."

At this time Victoria had not gained independence from New South Wales. In 1840 there was some discussion between pilotage authorities, Port Phillip pilots feeling they should be paid more than those at Port Jackson on account of the severity of the seas and the frequent gales of wind which persist in the bay at all periods of the year. Port Phillip pilots also made complaint that their earnings were insufficient to meet expenses.

An editorial in *The Herald* newspaper highlights their justifiable grievance:

"By reasonable exertions the Sydney pilots in the mere discharge of their duties netted a handsome income which by no means is too much for their fatigue, exertion, and danger they encounter.

But at Port Phillip the dangers are far greater, and it is not possible for them to earn a decent livelihood because, to begin with, they have to provide a boat and crew—at least four men at £4 a head—also each man has to construct his own residence. Moreover the trip up the bay is so long that no more than one trip a day can be made and they may have to wait for weeks for another vessel. In bad weather, even in the Bay, an open boat cannot live, and so how impossible is it to survive in the open sea.

At Sydney a pilot may take several vessels to an anchorage in a day and so a pilot's income is in the vicinity of £600 a year, whereas the Victorian pilots can hardly earn from £8 to £10 a month. We suggest that boats and crews be supplied to them which would mean a saving of £400 a year."

Superintendent La Trobe, later to be Lieutenant Governor, reacted favourably, and by the end of that year, after expenses on the pilot boats had been met, the sum to be divided between the six Port Phillip pilots was £2,591. With the gold rush, shipping increased to such an extent that, by 1854, 56 pilots were on the payroll at Port Phillip.

Western Australian pilotage functions under the Freemantle Harbour Trust, with three separate authorities, one being a private mining company. Prior to 1880 there were five pilots based in three different places.

In New Zealand, Dicky Barrett was engaged to pilot *The Tory* past the reef which now bears his name, into Wellington Harbour. This was one of New Zealand's first recorded acts of pilotage, and took place in 1839. In Auckland, pilotage started in 1840 when the Harbour Master was appointed as chief pilot. Two independent pilots were appointed in 1841, paying for their own boat and crew, and other services were established in 1874, 1877 and 1879, each controlled by the Harbour Board. Unlike most other countries, pilots have always been servants of the harbour boards, each Board being responsible for the development and safe operation of the port which it controls. It is the obligation of the Board to provide wharves, berthing, loading and unloading facilities, navigational aids, communications, dredging, marking and maintaining channels, and ensuring the safe and efficient working of the port, avoiding overcrowding.

The harbour master is the controlling officer for the port. Even in larger New Zealand ports, harbour masters undertake occasional pilotage, while pilots can be utilised to operate harbour board equipment when shipping movements are few in number. In contrast with many other countries, only a small number of ships are handled in a day in most New Zealand ports, yet there must be sufficient pilots to deal with peak periods.

The port of Hobart, capital port of Tasmania, with the largest "throughput" of cargo of all Tasmanian ports, had no harbour master or pilots until 1819, when Captain James Kelly was appointed the first official Harbour Master Pilot. Kelly knew the coastline well, having circumnavigated Tasmania in an open boat during 1815/16, accompanied by four convicts. Prior to that he had, for some years, been engaged in sealing voyages.

It is interesting to note that Kelly's appointment was made as a result of the theft of the schooner *Young Lachlan,* by a group of convicts.

By 1850, four pilots were employed, one of whom worked on a salaried basis, though he was only pilot for a year on account of limited trading. The other three pilots, with an average of 119 vessels a year requiring their services, divided their pilotage dues equally between them. The net result, however, could not have been substantial since they had to supply their own boat and crew, and house and feed them.

Among the European countries, France is notable inasmuch as the Sea Laws of France, established in 1681 by King Louis XIV, were the most comprehensive of all the ancient laws and ordinances. Besides being, to some extent, based on those of Rhodes, Oleron and the Hanseatic Laws, they bear a relationship to the laws of many modern maritime nations. Compulsory pilotage was prevalent in England almost from the beginning and spread throughout areas of maritime commerce in the old world during the seventeenth century.

Perhaps one of the most colourful histories of pilotage is that of the Hooghly River Pilots, now known as the Hooghly and Calcutta Pilot Service. It was the first truly international pilot service. Various changes in pilotage authority have taken place throughout the three centuries of its existence. The Bengal Service, to use its original name,

National Maritime Museum, London

East Indiaman homeward bound taking a pilot off Dover, 1800.

came into being in 1669 at the request of captains of the big East Indiamen. They carried precious British cargoes of lead and broadcloth and returned with silks, muslin and spices in exchange. Indian pilots were already operating, but were inexperienced in handling such large ships. Pirates were actively engaged on the river and rather than trust Indian pilots to navigate these valuable ships, with the risk of "accidental" grounding, arrangements were made for the cargo to be transported up the river in small country boats. Later, the 70-ton sloop, *Transport,* was purchased. Armed with a cannon, this vessel, under the command of William Bevis and his mate, George Becher, sailed from Balasore to Hooghly. This was the first ship to fly the British flag on this river.

In 1658 a British factory was established at Hooghly, but East Indiamen captains were still reluctant to pilot their vessels up this dangerous river. Additional pay was offered for the task and the pinnace, *Diligence,* was commissioned to "take notice of the channel and depth of the river Ganges and the entrance thereinto, to keep a journal, and to make exact drafts of their depths, reaches and currents and also how the sands usually vary."

Still the captains were not satisfied and insisted on having "able persons instructed as Pilots," adding, "for a supply of young men, to be bredd up wee have entertained as apprentices for seven years George Herron, James White, Thomas Massen, James Ferborne, John Ffloyd and Thomas Bateman."

These six men were Cinque Port pilots, well-known for their handling of ships in the London River. Their first task was to survey and chart the channels at the mouth of the Hooghly and to handle the Company's ships in and out. In 1679 George Herron prepared the first chart and issued sailing instructions.

A formal petition for the employment of these pilots was made to the Governor of Bengal, who gave the East India Company the privilege of bringing their ships up the Hooghly for the purpose of loading.

It was hardly surprising that ship masters were so insistent on the need for pilots. The river was so narrow in places that there was little room to pass even a comparatively small boat. Transit over the treacherous 125 miles up stream to Calcutta was stated to be one of the most difficult tasks a mariner could undertake. It was a river of bars, bores and bends. The draft, the tide, the navigation channel, the sandbars and the bends had to be "thoroughly studied, chewed and digested." Dense jungle spread from the banks on either side of the river and frequently ships had to be steered clear of the swollen carcases of wild animals which floated there. High winds sprang up without warning. Piloting a ship through the numerous bends and treacherous shoals was a constant struggle against nature.

In her book, *From Minnie with Love,* Jane Vansittart gives a colourful description of the end of the inward journey on the Hooghly:

"As the ship rounded the final curve, a forest of masts became visible against the hot, metallic sky, and behind them the magnificent outline of towers and minarets . . . The harbour was complete confusion, crammed as it was with boats, narrow 'flats' towing strings of barges, fishing boats, clipper ships, men-of-war, and a thousand small craft bent on their own concerns regardless of others. The noise was indescribable; yelling boatmen, the pilot bawling at craft blundering in his way, the sweating crew's bare feet thudding on the hot deck, the rattle of the chain as the anchor sank beneath the surface, and the ship was still at last."

Pilotage of the Hooghly became the best paid service in the world and the most unusual. No rates were laid down, pilots being reimbursed according to their skill. They appeared on the bridge wearing their white hats and immaculate navy blue swallow tail coats, with yellow braid, brass buttons all the way up the back, leather facings to lapels. They thought of themselves as gentlemen pilots of a very different class from the normal. They refused to eat the food prepared on the ship but arranged for their servants to cook sumptuous meals for them. They went down the river on outward bound ships and spent a few days on the pilot cutter before boarding a ship to pilot it on the inward journey. But they were well qualified for their work. Before piloting ships on the river a man must have served time in the Navy in marine survey; to have obtained his mate's certificate by the age of twenty, and served for five years as an apprentice.

Each pilot had his own brig and engaged in fierce competition to take ships up the river. They worked out in advance the maximum draught and claimed their fees on that basis.

Colourful and autocratic as these men were, they were most able navigators, bringing the big East Indiamen between the mouth of the river and Calcutta with a very high degree of safety. As their record of good pilotage increased so did their opinion of themselves. They had a retinue of Indian servants and considered themselves superior to any of the ship's officers below the rank of captain, while no passenger below the rank of Colonel dared engage them in conversation. In time, pilotage on the Hooghly River became so lucrative that directors of the East India Company were only too happy to encourage their relatives to undertake the exhaustive and rigorous training necessary to enter the service. Preference was given to boys of the Greenwich and Christ's Hospital Schools, and their descendants.

Rather less than two hundred years after the inception of official pilotage on the river there was a shortage of men in the Service. This resulted in officers of the merchant navy being engaged as pilots, after only half the normal length of training.

From that time conditions of entry changed many times until, more recently, the minimum qualification was amended to entry on a second mate's certificate with preference given to ex-cadets of the training ships *Worcester* and *Conway*.

Rudyard Kipling wrote:

"Almost any pilot will tell you that his work is more difficult than you imagine, but the Pilots of the Hooghly know that they have one hundred miles of the most difficult river on earth running through their hands, and they say nothing. Their service is picked and sifted as carefully as the bench of the Supreme Court, for a judge can only hang the wrong man—but a careless pilot can lose a 10,000 ton ship, with crew and cargo, in less time than it takes to reverse the engines."

What Kipling said of the problems of navigation on the Hooghly is true of many pilots who navigate today's tankers and ships carrying inflammable and explosive cargoes in narrow and difficult waters.

It was towards the end of the nineteenth century that the steamship began to replace the sailing ship on the Hooghly, with steamers being the only ships to sail up the entire length of the river.

Until the Second World War the service had been entirely British but due to the shortage of pilots during the war Indian pilots were recruited and have since given loyal service. Today, Indian officers possessing Second Mate's F.G. (Foreign Going) tickets can join the service.

In his message paying homage to the service on the occasion of its tercentenary, Captain B. S. Pavri, Harbour Master (River) and Branch Pilot, wrote:

"From 200 tons (D.W.) sailing vessels of 17th century, today the Pilot Service is handling and navigating vessels of 25,000 tons (D.W.) in narrow shallow and tidal waters of the Hooghly, and is prepared to handle ships of 100,000 tons (D.W.) which will use the river in the near future when Haldia Dock is commissioned.

I pay homage not only to the officers who are at present carrying on their responsible duties competently but also to those who handed down to us their rich experience and knowledge. I also pay homage to the staff of the Pilot Vessels, a part and parcel of the Pilotage Unit, who brave the hazards of the sea and are ever ready to ferry the pilots to and from ships at the head of the Bay of Bengal."

Another tribute, from the President of the Bengal Chamber of Commerce and Industry, states:

"In the three centuries which have elapsed since then (1669) the Pilots operating on the River Hoogly have acquired international fame and have been instrumental in developing Calcutta as one of the world's major ports . . . had the pilot service not acquired a complete mastery over the many hazards which the river presents, it is quite certain that Calcutta could never have grown to be one of the world's great industrial and commercial centres."

Cargo ships of many lands awaiting loading and unloading at Kidderpur Docks, Calcutta.
Information Services, High Commissioner of India, London

National Maritime Museum, London

Clearing a wreck—showing salvaging gear.

CHAPTER THREE

Wrecking, Plunder and Rescue

THAT there was not always the same concern for the safety of ships, their crews and cargo, is a fact of history; many are the stories told of wrecking and plunder, so prevalent in different parts of the world prior to the beginning of the nineteenth century. Some have been considerably embroidered, but official records confirm many shameful incidents. Any ship ashore was greeted with enthusiasm regardless of the loss of life incurred. As mentioned earlier, plundering was legal if no living creature came ashore and the attitude of coast dwellers all over the world was that anything thrown ashore from wrecks was "God's grace".

Lords of the manors in the southwestern regions of the British Isles were frequently involved in disputes with the Crown concerning the ownership of wrecks. These Lords had their rights in certain defined areas and employed armed retainers to defend them. On one occasion three such lords joined together to salvage goods from the wrecked *Gunwalloo* to the value of £10,000. The villagers, who considered they had equal rights to the plunder—and stood greatly in need of it—found it imperative to watch for such shipping disasters and arrive at the wreck before the lords or their retainers could get there. When a vessel went ashore off Helston in 1340 the villagers succeeded in removing everything on board, not only the cargo, but the whole of the ship's structure.

In *Cornish Shipwrecks—The South Coast,* Richard Larn describes the inhabitants of the eastern shore of Mount's Bay as having earned themselves the worst reputation for wrecking in the whole of Cornwall. He quotes from a letter written in 1710 which described the tinners of Germoe as "a mad people without fear of God or of the world who would cut a large trading vessel to pieces on one tide, strip half-dead men of their clothing, and cut down all who resist them."

No wonder mariners prayed that God would deliver them
"From Wicked Rocks and Shelving Sands
From Breague and Germoe men's hands."

On the other hand, the people of the Scilly Isles, whose coasts were as treacherous as any in that part of the country, offered a different prayer:

"We pray thee, O Lord, not that wrecks should happen, but that if any wrecks should happen, thou wilt guide them into the Scilly Isles for the benefit of the poor inhabitants."

Heath has described the interiors of the islanders' homes "as adorned with Saints' pictures, ears of corn and wreck furniture, the last of which are sent them by the Hand of Providence," further evidence of the prevailing attitude among coast dwellers at the time.

Although there are many stories of ships being lured to their doom by watchers on shore extinguishing beacons or bearing false lights, there is little evidence to substantiate these tales. There is one authenticated case of a lighthouse keeper in the Scilly Isles being sacked when he plundered a ship which had struck a rock before he had lit the fire in the lighthouse.

No service, however efficient and honourable, is without its black spots. Trustworthy as the Pilot Service is today, there were culprits even among these men. With Customs officers boarding vessels bound for Exmouth at the mouth of the Exe, it was difficult for any ship to be steered into the narrow entrance unobserved. Yet a rector of Littleham records that pilot boat crews took their opportunities to engage in smuggling. He writes:

"The presence of Customs officers did not deter Exmouth men from taking part in smuggling activities. The Exmouth pilot boats had special opportunities for smuggling, as they met incoming pilots off the Bar."

Liverpool pilots were thought not to be exempt from engaging in smuggling either. In 1764, before pilotage had been organised, and when pilots used their own boats, three pilot boats were seized by Customs officers because they were suspected of smuggling goods into the country from the Isle of Man.

Besides being accused of smuggling, pilots were not always as zealous in their duties as they are today. Records show that, in 1864, the master of an Exeter schooner anchored off Exmouth in a force ten wind, burnt flares to call a pilot, but without avail. Knowing the dangers of the narrow entrance to the Exe, especially at night, the master decided to shelter in Torbay, but the ship struck a rock near Dawlish. Although the crew was saved, the schooner broke up. At the resulting Board of Trade enquiry the pilots' defence was that "they never went to sea at all on such occasions."

Fourteen years later a disastrous wreck occurred as a result of the pilot's negligence in failing to set more canvas and sailing too close inshore while under the influence of drink.

The sailing vessel *Gossamer*—a famous full-rigged ship which had engaged in the annual tea races from Shanghai to London—was outward bound for Australia with valuable cargo. The pilot had come aboard at Gravesend, but because of the stormy weather the captain remained on deck for a day and two nights without sleep. When he did go to his cabin his sleep was interrupted by the chief mate informing him of the pilot's irresponsible behaviour. Not only was there serious loss of life when the ship hit some rocks and broke up, but thousands of pounds worth of cargo was stolen by the wreckers from the villages around Prawle, Salcombe and Torcross. A well-known farmer of that area even brought his labourers to help with the pickings, as a result of which they were all sent for trial at Kingsbridge. At the local sessions the pilot who had been responsible for the wreck was found guilty of manslaughter, but the result of the further trial at local assize is unknown.

Although there are these and other early reports of inefficient and untrustworthy pilots, there were many more examples of courage and bravery in rescuing ship-wrecked mariners. Often pilots faced a sea that seemed to others to offer nothing but sudden death; many pilots did, in fact, lose their lives in their attempts at rescue.

The Essex coast had its share of gallant rescues. Often these took place when other shipping was seeking shelter. Robert Malster, in his book *Wreck and Rescue on the Essex Coast,* tells a gripping story of the scene when the London brig *Lochiel* foundered in a gale and "was stripped of stores and gear" before the eyes of her master and crew. At daybreak, after the vessel had been a night on the sands, eight smacks came up and the smacksmen boarded the brig. Finding their efforts at jettisoning the cargo and pumping her out were unavailing, Captain Garrick decided to send his crew off in the smacks' boats, but said later:

"We were told by the smacksmen that, in consequence of their boats being so small and the weather so bad, they could take only a few of their most valuable things, which was done, and put into the boats, leaving our other things on board in the hope of the weather moderating enough to afford us a chance of recovering them. But as soon as we had placed our things in the boat, the other smacksmen that were on board went down below, breaking open the chests and lockers, and taking things out of them, and loading their boats, with the exception of Captain E. Eagle, master of the smack *George and Eliza*, of Colchester, and Captain Andrews, of the smack *Fair Traveller*, also of Colchester, who would take nothing but what belonged to the men they had to take off and endeavoured to take as many of my things with them as possible. They frequently reprimanded the other men for taking and appropriating to their own use the clothes of the shipwrecked sailors."

Captain Garrick went aboard one of the smacks, which proceeded into Sheerness for shelter. When they returned to the wreck next morning he found her stripped of everything except the lower and topmast standing rigging.

Not only were ships pillaged by some salvagers, in one case they actually lit a fire to warm themselves in the cabin, resulting in the ship catching fire.

On the other hand occasionally the very men who took risks to effect rescues were falsely accused of unlawfully retaining stores and materials, such as the mainsail, a topsail, squaresail and a quantity of rope which had been picked up by the rescuers at sea. Malster, reporting this particular case adds: "In spite of the fact that the gear had been landed almost as soon as they came into port, and they had declared their intention of reporting it as soon as the Receiver's office opened next morning, the men were convicted and fined fifteen guineas each, double the value of the articles seized."

A further instance quoted by Malster in the same book shows the tenacity and devotion to duty displayed by these smacksmen, in this case from Colchester:

"The brig *Traveller* had gone ashore on the Gunfleet in a howling gale. When the two Colchester smacks went to her aid the next morning (Sunday) she was breaking up. The crew had taken to the rigging and although the smacks stood by all day they could not get near enough to effect a rescue. All they could do was to signal to the men, suffering intensely on the rigging, that they would not abandon them. With improved weather the next morning, ten of the men were rescued after being in the rigging for thirty hours with limbs so swollen that their clothes had to be cut away."

CHAPTER FOUR

Development of Ports and Harbours

BOTH commercial and public interest demand that the conduct of vessels in the confined waters of harbours and the adjacent seas should be in the hands of experienced mariners who have a detailed knowledge of the locality and the dangers which may exist. Although navigation aids have been greatly extended and improved throughout the years, as have harbours and docking facilities, the need for pilots is as great, if not greater than it ever was.

In the Report of the Commission of Enquiry on Harbour Pilotage in New Zealand, dated May, 1975, the Commissioners investigating the need for pilots found that:

"The danger to a vessel of grounding and being stranded or wrecked increases as it approaches closer to land. Similarly, the risk of collision with other vessels or objects is increased when the vessel is manoeuvring in confined waters."

Without efficient ports, the trade upon which most countries' existence depends would not be a viable proposition. Therefore, as the New Zealand Commissions Report suggests, "it would be a national disaster if one of the major ports was closed to shipping due to a casualty which blocked entry to the port or otherwise caused cessation of normal harbour activity." This is equally true of most countries throughout the world.

A brief description of the development of some of the ports in different parts of the world, is, therefore, relevant to a book of this nature, enabling the reader better to understand the problems, responsibilities and need for today's pilots.

Following the Industrial Revolution in England towards the end of the eighteenth century, and the expansion of foreign trade, ports and harbours, docks and quays were enlarged and improved in the main coastal towns in the British Isles until today many small towns have become world ports of great importance, handling vast quantities of cargo in great variety. Since this has resulted in the ever increasing size and type of ships, it has had a direct bearing on pilotage until it has become the highly organised service of today.

Originally ports were built as high up the river as was consistent with the size of the ships using the port; this was done as a protection against invaders. Ships were small so ports were often a long way from the sea. When shipping began increasing in size and quantity docks were built nearer the sea. Tilbury, which serves London, is a case in point.

With the growth of local trades and industries, each port had its special characteristics; for example, those ports concerned mainly with fishing needed different facilities from those in South Wales and other places where coal was the main export commodity, while the larger towns, catering for many kinds of cargo, required a more diversified docking area.

An aerial view of the new £50 million Royal Seaforth Dock, Liverpool. On the left the grain terminal and on the right the four-berth container terminal with 65 acres of stacking space.

The Mersey Docks and Harbour Board

The early history of Liverpool is not clear, but it is likely that the great seaport of today began as a small town clustered round its natural harbour, "The Pool". The creek on the east bank of the River Mersey ran inland from a point just south of the present Pier Head as far as today's entrance to the first Mersey Tunnel. From 1207, when King John, the real founder of the City and Port, granted a charter giving the town Borough status, its population and commerce gradually developed. By 1533 a visitor to the town was able to report—"Irish merchants come much hither as to a good haven" and that there was "much Irish yarn that Manchester do buy."

As trade developed proposals to improve the pool were put forward, though little progress was made until the Corporation decided, in the reign of Queen Anne, to "render the Harbour safe by art as the other great commercial Ports of the Kingdom were by nature." After considerable opposition the first commercial wet dock in England was built on a four-acre site at the mouth of the Pool, but construction work was not completed until 1720.

From that time the port developed rapidly, other docks being built during the eighteenth century while, by the end of the American War of Independence, the increase in trade was so rapid that further docks were needed. From that time until the present day there has been a continuing expansion in the port to meet the changing needs of shipping and trade. The only events which have halted the progress of the port were the Napoleonic Wars and the First and Second World Wars.

Queen Elizabeth II Dock, Eastham, Manchester Ship Canal. *Port of Manchester*

In the late eighteenth and nineteenth centuries, a succession of Parliamentary Acts extended the docks north and south along the Lancashire coast, as well as at Birkenhead on the Wirral. This was done in order to deal with the demands for food and raw materials, while, as British trade increased, the products of factories and mills were sent throughout the world.

During the Victorian era 34 docks were constructed in the port to give deeper water and longer quays to match the changing design of ships. Deep water river entrances allowed vessels to dock and undock at any state of the tide and a floating stage half a mile long, known as the Princes Landing Stage, was built for the passenger trade. The climax seemed to have been reached with the opening of the Gladstone Dock System, then the biggest and deepest docks in the world.

Since the Second World War there has been a continuous programme of modernisation, with the new buildings and port equipment, such as floating cranes and dredgers, while a new river entrance lock and seven modern cargo berths were opened in 1962. Culmination of this vast programme of expansion of the Port of Liverpool was reached in July, 1973, when the Royal Seaforth Dock was opened. It was one of the largest single dock projects in Europe since the war, with facilities for grain, meat, timber and forest products, together with a fully computerised container terminal based on a site of 500 acres reclaimed from the Mersey, leaving room for further expansion as required.

Closely linked with the Mersey by the Manchester Ship Canal is the Port of Manchester, which was opened to traffic on New Year's Day 1894, converting an inland city into a port. As a port for ocean-going vessels the city is able to send its commodities direct to countries overseas. Imported goods include petroleum, ores, grain, woodpulp, sand and gravel, timber, metals, paper, foodstuffs, chemicals, cotton, iron and steel and clay. The Queen Elizabeth II Dock at Eastham, opened in January 1954, is stated to be the largest of its kind in the country. It has its own entrance lock, 807 feet long by 100 feet wide, and can accommodate four large tankers at one time. The Manchester Ship Canal has brought the sea to Manchester with all the advantages of deep water transport to a large inland area, giving it a premier position in industry and commerce, but it would not be the busy and progressive place it is today had the pilotage service not co-operated with the port. With over 5,000 ships entering the waterway each year, bearing over 16,000,000 tons of cargo, Liverpool and Manchester pilots have to be highly organised to bring them safely to their destination.

Glasgow was established in early times on the banks of a river at the lowest point at which a bridge could be built. At the beginning of the eighteenth century the people of the city were engaged chiefly in fishing, sugar refining and the manufacture of soap and cloth. Trade was mostly with Ireland and England, with a limited foreign trade with Holland and France. The harbour consisted of a water area of about two and a half acres, the quayage extending for about 262 yards on the north bank of the river to the west. With the river little more than a broad and shallow stream and flowing westward away from the direction of foreign trade, Glasgow was handicapped as the centre of commerce. The depth of water at the harbour was only fifteen inches at low tide and less than four feet at high water, with

General view of Tees Dock.

Trojan Photographic, Middlesbrough

numerous shoals and fords in the river and small islands dividing the channel, so that overseas vessels could not make the passage to Glasgow.

The trading position improved considerably following the Union of the English and Scottish Parliaments in 1707, when the English Colonies were opened to Scottish traders. The geographical position of Glasgow and the Clyde was now in a specially advantageous position to engage in the prosperous tobacco trade with Maryland, Virginia and the Carolinas. Sailing vessels engaged in this trade could make the return voyage to America and back in four to six weeks less than vessels out of other Scottish and English ports. By 1720 there was a regular weekly sailing from the Clyde, and forty years later Glasgow was handling more than half of Britain's total imports of tobacco.

Yet the lack of deep water in the river still prevented ocean-going vessels from making the trip direct, foreign cargoes being discharged at Port Glasgow and Dumbarton. Trade with the Colonies at that time was mostly by barter which created a demand for home produced goods and necessitated full outward cargoes to leave from the Clyde. As a result merchants developed other industries and began to manufacture linen and cotton goods, leather, rope, glass and pottery.

At this time it was realised that improvements must be made to the river in order that larger vessels could proceed to Glasgow. Parliament therefore gave the Town Council powers to "cleanse, straighten, enlarge and improve the river from Dumbuck Ford above Dumbarton to the Bridge of Glasgow," and authorisation was given for dues to be charged on vessels and goods using the river. Eventually 117 jetties were built projecting into the river at right angles from both banks. This increased the natural scour of the river and, together with the dredging put into operation, was so effective that, within two years, vessels drawing six feet were arriving and departing from Broomielaw at high tide. Though a small increase in depth compared with later developments, it proved that greater results could be achieved with the provision of sufficient money and additional effort.

As in so many other cases, the American War of Independence caused a severe setback to Glasgow's trade until they embarked on trade with the West Indies, developing the cotton industry, later to become so prosperous. With the exploitation of the coal and blackband ironstone at the beginning of the nineteenth century Glasgow entered the era of heavy industry and engineering.

The Industrial Revolution, which brought great changes in shipping and transport generally, resulted in further work being done to deepen the river until vessels of 17 feet draught could be accommodated comfortably at Broomielaw. Sailing ships gave way to steam, wooden vessels to iron and later to steel and the railway system began. The application of steam power to dredging, which previously had been done by means of dragging ploughs and harrow along the bed of the river and tossing the silt and mud on to the banks, greatly accelerated the improvement of the channel. In 1975 a feasibility study with ship designers and builders was started to provide Clydeport with a new vessel to meet all the port's dredging needs, enabling the existing dredging fleet to be replaced by one large grab hopper-dredger. It is anticipated that the new hopper-dredger will be equipped with three or four large grab-cranes and also a suction pipe unit and be capable of carrying about 2,000 cubic metres of dredged material.

As the depth of navigable water increased, additional quays were built to provide more berthage, but the Clyde Navigation Trustees, who were then responsible for the management of that part of the river, realised that sufficient riverside berthage could not be provided. In consequence the Trustees embarked upon the construction of docks. During the following forty years Queen's Dock, Prince's Dock and Rothesay Dock were built, the latter being the first dock in the world with all electrically operated equipment. King George V Dock was opened in 1931.

Shipbuilding on the Clyde was practically non-existent until after the War of Independence. Until then ships engaged in trade with North America had either been chartered from owners at Whitehaven or, for the most part, been built in America. With the deepening of the navigable channel of the Clyde, there was a great upsurge in shipping and shipbuilding on the river. Big shipping companies came into being and began trading all over the world. These shipping companies wished to engage pilots known to them and thus a class of Special, or Choice pilots came into being and exists in Clyde pilotage to this day, as it does in London, Southampton, Liverpool and some other ports, a matter which has occasionally caused a certain amount of dissatisfaction and dissension among some pilots.

At the present time Clydeport handles in one year about 15,000 vessels and 18,000,000 tons of goods, including two-thirds of all foreign trade through Scottish ports. With its designated 450 square miles of water it contains many port facilities which are equal to those anywhere else in the world. Meadowside Granary is the largest single grain storage unit in Great Britain, with grain coming from ports in Australia, Canada, the U.S.A. and Russia, in vessels ranging from large bulk carriers to general cargo ships with small parcels. A record cargo of 27,335 tons of maize from South Africa was discharged from the bulk carrier *Kirriemoor* in a little over three working days. The Iron Ore/Coal Terminal, Container Terminal, Sugar Berth, Tanker Berth, Roll-on/Roll-off Services and Dockyard, all suggest that Clydeport has need of fully trained pilots to conduct ships safely on their inward and outward journeys, and there are still more plans for expansion, with the proposed further reclamation of land at Hunterston.

Middlesborough Dock, on the south bank of the Tees, handles over 800,000 tons of cargo a year, the largest tonnages being chemicals and fertilisers, iron and steel and petroleum products. Ships are able to enter the dock from two and a quarter hours before, to one and a half hours after high water, while immediately inside the dock gates there is a swinging area which enables vessels to enter and leave the dock bow first. The depth of water on the outer sill of the dock allows vessels of up to 17,500 dwt* with a maximum beam of 23.2 m to be handled.

As in other ports mentioned, development of the port and its facilities for the smooth entry and turn-around of today's ships, and the handling of their cargo, is continually in

*See notes at end of chapter.

Aerial view of Saltend Oil Terminal, Hull.   *British Transport Docks Board, Hull*

progress. At Seal Sands over 400 acres of land have been reclaimed recently for the Phillips North Sea Oil development. Dredging has also been completed for a fifty-acre inset dock and work on four crude oil berths and four smaller berths for gas carriers made it possible for the first oil to be brought ashore in 1975. Reclamation of land and extension of plant are still proceeding in the area.

Hull, known especially for its trawler fleet of over 100 vessels, is a regular port of call for ocean-going and short sea vessels carrying a great variety of general cargo. Its wide clear quays are backed by covered and open storage; there are floating and shore suction elevators for the handling of the vast quantity of grain imported, and ten different terminals for unit loading. This assists with the speedy turn-around for ships engaging in trade with vital world markets, in particular, with Scandinavian and other Continental countries. King George and Queen Elizabeth Docks have seven roll-on/roll-off berths. Four are engaged with passenger and freight traffic to and from Holland and Belgium, while the other three are the points of departure and entry for sailings to and from Finland, Sweden, Denmark and Norway. These countries, as well as East and West Germany, are also served by the lift-on/lift-off container terminal. At Salt End two deep water oil jetties extend 487.7m out into the Humber and carry pipeline connections to nearby tank farms, which have a total capacity well in excess of 681,900,000 litres. Passenger/freight vessels, used by North Sea Ferries between Hull and Rotterdam and Zeebrugge, are the largest of their type in the world.

Mechanical handling equipment, conveyor systems and all the latest facilities for unloading, processing and marketing, ensure speedy discharge of the catch from the fishing fleet which brings over a quarter of the total frozen and fresh fish for the British Isles.

Research and planning continues for further development and equipment to meet the demands of future commerce.

At the entrance to the Schelde is Flushing Roads, about forty-eight miles from Antwerp, one of the busiest stretches of water used by sea-going vessels. There sea pilots and Schelde pilots take over from each other. This changeover causes ships to slow down, thereby leading to delays and congestion, especially in bad weather, which creates difficult manoeuvring situations. The original Ghent Canal, cut in the sixteenth century, was developed between 1900 and 1910 with considerable further development starting in 1960. New locks were built for the use of ships 250m in length and a new entrance harbour from the Schelde, 1500m long and 250m wide, was constructed with dolphin berths for ships requiring emergency moorings or waiting for locks.

Rotterdam was originally a village of fisherfolk and farmers, it grew into a small town with its first permanent settlement developing in 1270 when a dam was thrown across the River Rotte. This provided the only link with the surrounding country until the Rotterdamsche Schie Canal was dug in 1348 connecting the town with the Province of North and South Holland. The development of Rotterdam really began with the granting of its charter in 1340 by William IV, Count of Holland. The country was important to the maritime trade of Europe but the silting of the Meuse caused a large sandbank to build up.

Belgian pilot boat at the Flushing Station where Schelde River Pilots are exchanged for Sea Pilots and vice versa.
D. A. McDonald

By the beginning of the sixteenth century this had become a tremendous drawback to trade, ships having to take devious roundabout routes to reach Rotterdam. The increasing size of ships thwarted such attempts as were made to overcome this problem until a canal was cut right through the sand dunes to the Hook of Holland. On 31st October, 1866, work on the canal began. It proved to be a four-year task and even then another two years had to be spent in deepening the canal before the New Waterway could be fully operative. The industrialisation of the Rhur emphasised the importance of its ideal situation at the heart of the Rhine Delta, with the Rhine the most inexpensive highroad to the sea. New sea docks were necessary to keep pace with this changed situation, and these were built on the left bank of the Meuse. By the end of the nineteenth century the population of Rotterdam had tripled, shipping increased, Rotterdam thrived and the docks grew with an increasing number of pilots required to service ships using the port.

Then came the Second World War, the blackest period in Rotterdam's history. The centre of the city was reduced to a mass of smoking rubble; thousands of people were killed and thousands more made homeless, but such was the spirit of the people that plans were drawn for a new city.

Following the war, with the increasing importance of oil, new refineries were constructed on the South Bank and on Rozenburg Island, attracting the petrochemical industry. Then came the closure of the Suez Canal resulting in the oil companies building larger tankers. Europort docks were deepened and an eight mile channel dredged from

Europort to the Maasbuoy (pilot cutter) and beyond that the Eurochannel is sixteen miles into the North Sea, thus creating the whole new area of Maasvlakte, off Rozenburg Island. A large container centre was built but even this proved inadequate to deal with the revolution in general cargo traffic brought about by the rise of containerisation, and plans were put in hand for a further development on the northern bank of the New Waterway. When this is completed it is expected to give a dock complex capable of handling every modern method of transportation.

Rotterdam has become an international distribution centre, the major bulk carrier port of the world, fully mechanised, more than 45,000,000 tons of cargo being handled annually. A network of pipelines connects the leading oil industries of Amsterdam, Antwerp and Western Germany with the Rotterdam-Europort unloading and storage facilities.

Covering 14,800 acres, nearly a third of which are harbour basins and canals, Europort has access for ships of 300,000 dwt, with a draught of sixty-eight feet.

In spite of, and partly because of all that has been done to make Rotterdam such a vital port, technological change continues. Developments in hovercraft are likely to lead to the operation of cargo-carrying hovercraft on the North Sea. Rotterdam's multi-million-pound Rijnport plan provides for handling unit-load carrying hovercraft as well as container and roll-on/roll-off vessels. Over 31,000 seagoing vessels and over 250,000 inland craft call at this junction of world traffic every year, most of which are handled by Rotterdam pilots.

All over the world ports have been enlarged and re-equipped and their waters deepened with the advance in cargo handling and the ever increasing size of ships. One of many such examples is the Port of Hobart, in Tasmania. Since 1804 this port has grown steadily from a tree-lined cove to the neat expanse of wharfage and cargo handling facilities which exists today, its 20 deep water berths now dealing with about 2,000,000 tons of cargo

Two pilot cutters in the Schelde entrance.

Royal Netherlands Navy

annually, with the capacity to increase this figure. Instead of the wooden piling used in the construction of Kings Pier, the Empress of Australia terminal is of prestressed concrete and has modern cargo handling facilities. Hobart is a natural harbour, its depths of water, sheltered anchorages and scenic beauty being comparable to Sydney and Rio de Janeiro. The small amount of siltation which takes place necessitates no great amount of dredging, while a good anchorage is afforded to vessels in bad weather because of the rock formation, with its thick layer of heavy mud, which covers most of the sea bed.

The apple season involves the port in its busiest time, but there is a steady flow of coastal traffic throughout the year, with overseas vessels bringing imports necessary to Tasmanian industry.

Besides the facilities which exist for large overseas vessels there are berths for roll-on/roll-off container vessels and oil tankers, while the export of manufactured zinc and the import of zinc concentrates and phosphate rock are handled from the River Derwent. 36,000 ton bulk carriers deal with the 600,000 tons of wood chips shipped to Japan annually. Murray Street Pier is concerned with the maintenance and upkeep of craft used by the Marine Board, including the pilot vessel, patrol boat, tugs and other working craft. At the Dock Head Building, radio watch on vessels entering, leaving or manoeuvring in the harbour is continuous.

The Marine Board of Hobart is responsible for the administration of the port, its members (known as Wardens) representing importers, exporters and shipowners.

All these ports and their facilities for seagoing traffic, and the discharge of their cargo, are indicative of the importance which the speedy and safe shipment of goods holds to the world's trade today.

Gross tonnage	=	ship's volume, not weight
1 Gross ton	=	100 cubic feet of enclosed space including engine room, fuel tanks, cargo holds, bridge, sleeping quarters, passageways, galley, game rooms, etc.
Net tonnage	=	cargo space.
1 ton	=	100 cubic feet.
		(*dwt*)
Deadweight tonnage	=	2,240 lbs.
1 long ton	=	Measure of weight including cargo, stores, water, bunker (fuel) and crew members.

A ship's dwt is the weight that will bring it down to the Plimsoll Line — the legal limit for loading.

ms *Winston Churchill*, 8,661 tons.

DFDS

CHAPTER FIVE

Navigation and Safety Aids

SEAMARKS of one kind or another have always been a necessary and important aid to navigation, the best known probably being lighthouses. These were established along the trade routes of the Hanseatic League towards the end of the Middle Ages, but they did not exist to any great extent on the English coast until the eighteenth century. Buoys and a primitive type of beacon came first, though for many years landmarks were the most reliable means of ensuring a safe passage for coastal vessels and ships entering or leaving ports, the principal marks being windmills and churches. These were of such importance that, in 1566, an Act was passed by Parliament forbidding the destruction or alteration of such marks. Mariners and pilots were still very dependent on landmarks in the nineteenth century, as is evidenced by a letter from the Brethren of Hull Trinity House to the vicar of Killingholme Church, in which they asked that he cut down the trees in front of his church "as they prevented it being used as a seamark as it has been for a great number of years." The vicar was informed that he could be fined one hundred pounds for failing to comply. In the event it was found that the trees in question were owned by two other gentlemen who had agreed to remove them.

A few years later the Brethren of Hull Trinity House expressed themselves as willing to "donate one hundred pounds towards the erection of a spire on St James's Church in Hull." Although this was never put into effect, the accounts show that Trinity House did pay seven shillings and sixpence for whitewashing a house at Paull to make it more obvious to those at sea.

Beacons of many kinds were erected at different times on land and on the sea-bed, most of which were frequently in need of resetting and repair. In 1647 the Brethren arranged with a Paull boatman to set up and maintain the Burcom beacon, the first having been so badly damaged that it had to be replaced. A fir pole about thirty feet long was to be provided by Trinity House, the length being required to ensure that it was always visible whatever the state of the tide. The sand dried out at low water, which was probably why sixteen tons of stones were deposited at the base to give it support against tides and waves.

Two hundred years later major replacements of seamarks took place on the Lower Humber, including the renewal of the Kilnsea beacon which had been repaired on several occasions already. It was now suffering from sea erosion to such an extent that it was standing only sixteen yards from the cliff edge and to avoid its being washed away altogether it was moved further inland.

Buoys are set to warn mariners of shallow water, wrecks and other dangers. By their shapes and colours they indicate the safe channels, and mark routes for specific purposes, such as the two-way traffic separation in the Straits of Dover through which approximately 300 ships a day pass, making it one of the most heavily congested seaways in the world. With the opening of the scheme in 1971, following a number of disastrous collisions, additional buoys were laid and a new light vessel station established in 1972. The French Lighthouse Service was responsible for changes to seamarks for the north-bound lane and Trinity House, London for the south-bound lane.

In the same year Trinity House, in co-operation with the Port of London Authority, provided and laid buoys for a new deep water approach to the Port of London. This was necessitated by the increasing size and draught of modern oil tankers and bulk carriers. 23 lighted buoy stations were installed and others discontinued, moved or re-named.

For well over three hundred years Trinity House has maintained unlighted buoys. An Act passed in 1566 empowered the Corporation to supervise seamarks throughout England, though little appears to have been done about this and there was doubt as to whether the Act provided for the laying of buoys and beacons in the water itself. The Act passed in 1594, however, gave them full powers to undertake the beaconage and buoyage of the Thames, a task for which they were well qualified by their constant use of the river. Regular inspection of seamarks became necessary with the passing of the Act and agents were appointed at different times to attend to this. Not only was repositioning of buoys sometimes necessary but it was occasionally considered desirable to replace a beacon with a buoy and vice versa.

Early buoys were mostly made of wood and bound by iron hoops. These were moved with the changing of the sands, with additional buoys and lights being found necessary from time to time. Today's buoys are of mild steel or wrought iron, varying in diameter from five feet to twelve feet and weighing from three to twelve tons without moorings; some carry whistles, bells and sometimes small electric fog signals. The majority are fitted with radar reflectors to make them more easily identifiable on ships' radar.

The beginnings of a uniform system of buoyage emerged in 1889, when certain countries agreed to mark the port hand side of channels with black conical buoys and the starboard hand side with red conical buoys.

Unfortunately, when lights for buoys were introduced, some European countries placed red lights on the black port hand buoys to conform with the red lights marking the port hand side of harbour entrances, whilst throughout North America, red lights were placed on the red starboard hand buoys.

Thereafter various conferences were convened which sought for a single buoyage system, but without success until 1936 when another uniform system of buoyage was formulated in a Convention drawn up under The League of Nations at Geneva. It established a cardinal system, and a lateral system with the principle that red lights and red buoys should be used on the port hand, and white lights and black buoys on the starboard hand. But several countries, including the U.S.A. were not signatories to this convention and continued to develop their original, and opposite, system.

The Convention, however, was still unratified when most European buoyage systems were swept away by the Second World War (1939-45). After the war buoyage systems were re-established in north-west Europe based on the 1936 Geneva Convention, but with wide differences in interpretation, which has led to nine different systems being used in these waters.

Shifting sands, causing channels to become shallow and dangerous for larger ships, resulted in shipowners petitioning the Corporation to attend to this; in one case shipowners offered to pay ten pence per hundred tons on all inward bound ships to meet the cost of installation and maintenance of the necessary sea marks. One of the problems of the use of buoys was that they tended to break away from their moorings in bad weather. This created a dangerous situation because masters navigating their vessels through the shoals anticipated that they could rely on the buoy being in its correct position.

In 1833 concern about navigation into Liverpool resulted in the Admiralty ordering a survey of the North Wales coast and Liverpool Bay as a result of which the New Channel was buoyed, lighted and later dredged, enabling vessels to use the port whatever the state of the tide. Prior to that time Liverpool was only a half tide port, which caused the delay of about 260 Dublin mail boats annually. Today the Mersey Docks and Harbour Company maintains over one hundred buoys.

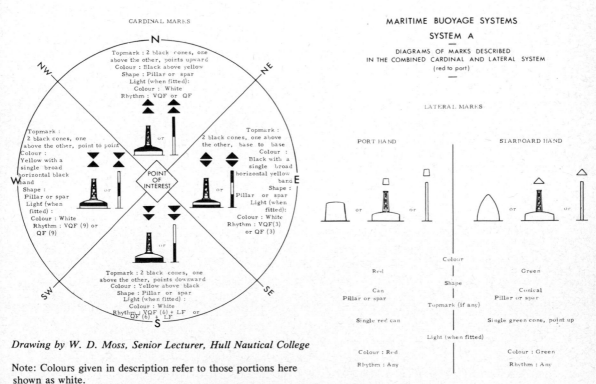

Drawing by W. D. Moss, Senior Lecturer, Hull Nautical College

Note: Colours given in description refer to those portions here shown as white.

International Association of Lighthouse Authorities

The first gas lighted buoy to be used in the Lower Humber had a speedy and disastrous end when the buoy capsized in a severe storm and the lantern was lost. However, following the storm the buoy was repaired, the height of the pedestal reduced by three feet and a new lantern fitted, the cost being thirty-two pounds. From then on the main buoys of the river were replaced by lighted buoys.

Recently an International Committee was set up by the International Association of Lighthouse Authorities (I.A.L.A.) to find a way to overcome the problems created by the multiplicity of National Maritime Buoyage Systems in use throughout the world. More than thirty systems exist at present, nine of which are in North West Europe. For a number of years the Association had this problem before them and the obvious need to mark wrecks in busy waterways such as the Dover Straits and English Channel made it necessary for some attempt to be made to solve the difficulty. Serving as Chairman and Secretary were a member of Trinity House Board and a member of the staff of Trinity House, with representatives from North West Europe, Canada and the U.S.A. on the committee. The Committee's brief was to formulate simple, easy to remember rules, using existing equipment as far as possible to reduce cost.

It soon became apparent to the Committee that it would not be possible to have one single world-wide system and it was decided to aim for two: System A to be used in Europe, Africa, India, Australia and most of Asia; System B being used on the North and South American Continents, the Caribbean and parts of Asia.

The proposed new System A, known as the Combined Lateral and Cardinal System, utilises principles well known to mariners, where, in well defined channels, green buoys with green lights will mark the starboard and red buoys with red lights the port.

The Committee recommend that outlying and well separated dangers should be marked by Cardinal buoys indicating to the mariner the compass direction in which he can find the best water. Cardinal buoys, which are black and yellow, with distinctive topmarks, are those which rely by night on very easy to distinguish flashing white lights, as mentioned earlier.

All dangers, including wrecks, would be marked in a similar fashion, and the mariner would have to learn only ten simple rules instead of the multiplicity of conflicting rules now in use.

To enable the Hydrographic Chart Makers to produce the new charts needed by the mariner, the Committee recommend the new system should be introduced progressively over a period of several years.

The first stage of the new system, which it is proposed should commence on 14th April, 1977, will be in one of the most congested areas in the world. On the United Kingdom side this is from about Newhaven on the South Coast through the Dover Straits to Orfordness on the East Coast. A similar stretch of the French and Belgian Coasts will be dealt with concurrently, over a period of three to four months.

The second stage, to commence in the spring of 1978, will deal with the remainder of the East Coasts of the United Kingdom, while the third stage will commence in 1979 and deal with the South and West Coasts of the United Kingdom and Ireland.

PLA Survey Boat *Havengore*. This craft undertakes work in regard to Conservancy including attention to buoys and lights.
Port of London Authority

Light vessels could be described as floating lighthouses. They are shaped to withstand bad weather and are securely moored in position near dangerous sandbanks where lighthouses could not be built. The light is on a tower in the centre of the vessel.

Arthur Storey, in his history of *Pilotage and Navigational Aids of the River Humber (1512-1908)* records that, in 1832, consideration was given to the idea of having a floating light in the form of a wooden vessel of 100 tons anchored at the mouth of the river. Estimates showed that it would cost £1,000 to build and £600 a year to operate. The project was acceptable and the Admiralty notice concerning this, dated 3rd January, 1833, reads:

"A floating light vessel is moored off the south east end of Hull Sand. Bright light exhibited from a single lantern on the evening of the 1st instant. Shows a blue flag during daytime and in hazy and dark weather a gong is sounded." Later a bell was used instead of the gong when visibility was restricted.

Storey records that "the crew consisted of the master, mate and four seamen, one of whom was paid an extra five shillings per month" for tending the lantern. Letters from the master of this light vessel tell how the mooring chain was "payed out" in stormy weather to give better holding with the changing force of the wind. Rolling and straining in heavy seas, the vessel shipped water, which caused the caulking of the ship's sides to open and the lantern to leak. The lifeboat men at Spurn, as servants of the Corporation, were paid three pounds three shillings to put twelve tons of sand and gravel into the light vessel as ballast, while carpenters were sent from Hull to repair the damage caused by ships colliding with the light vessel when manoeuvring near it.

The importance attached to the problem of navigating the Lower Humber, with the frequent alteration of the course, is shown by the fact that, in 1860, the Brethren at Hull

Trinity House were maintaining five shore lights, two lightships, thirty buoys and four beacons. Yet, in spite of all these navigational aids, vessels collided with buoys and lightships, fourteen buoys being damaged and five broken adrift in a period of three months in 1866.

Arthur Storey, in his book mentioned earlier in this chapter, records the following dramatic incident which took place that year, severely damaging the lightship:

"On September 7th, the Prussian barque *Emma Johanna,* hit the lightship. The anchor of the barque, which was hanging from the hawsepipe, holed the lightship below the water-line and the mast rigging and lantern were damaged. When the crew realised that their vessel was sinking they hailed a nearby tug, connected the towline, slipped the moorings and made for Grimsby. The vessel 'made' water quicker than the pumps got rid of it and she had to be run on to the mud a quarter of a mile below Grimsby piers to prevent her sinking. When the buoy master heard of the accident he ordered the spare lightship at Hull to be got ready, manned and taken to the Bull sand. Meantime he proceeded to Grimsby. He realised that the spare lightship would not reach the mouth of the river until the following day, so he arranged for a fishing smack to moor at the Bull sand, to act as a temporary lightship for the night until the arrival of the spare lightship. In his report later submitted to the board he tells of raising the vessel and getting it to Hull. He proceeded to the wrecked lightship on the mud and at low water, when the mud flats were practically dry, he inspected the damaged hull. It was a quick inspection as the rising tide soon surrounded the vessel and by high water time it was twelve feet under water. Next, he made arrangements to plug the hole and to start lifting the vessel next morning. Eight pumps were hired together with men to tackle the job. Salvage operations started just before low water the following day but as the tide did not leave the vessel entirely dry two men had to work in water to plug the hole in the hull. After this was done, the pumps started to operate in an effort to get the water out of the hull before the tide covered the vessel again. It was a near thing as the vessel lifted just as the tide was nearly level with the deck. A tug was connected and with the pumping continuing the tow set off for Hull. As it was realised that the plug might work loose and the vessel start leaking, the vessel was kept in shallow water so that she could be beached if necessary. All went well and when the tow arrived in Hull the lightship was immediately placed on the Dock Company's gridiron in Victoria Dock basin. The repairs were completed on September 26th. The following day the lightship was towed to the Bull Sand, moored on her station and the spare lightship was brought back to Hull."

For over three hundred years Trinity House of Kingston-upon-Hull established and maintained navigational aids on the Lower Humber. In 1906 the Humber Conservancy Board took over control of the Upper and Lower Humber and navigational aids were handed over to that Board.

There are now three light vessels marking the Goodwin Sands, the crews of which are responsible for keeping their vessels in their correct position. Altogether there are about 24 light vessels under the control of Trinity House, London, with several in reserve. This is the largest fleet of light vessels in the world. They are mainly positioned at major and strategic navigational points along the East Coast of England, in the North Sea, each having a crew of five men who work duty periods of a month on/month off. Due to the high cost of maintenance of these vessels consideration is being given to the possibility of replacing some of them with fixed structures and the use of Large Automatic Buoys (LANBY) where a floating seamark is essential because the navigational hazard is not always at the same place. The buoy in question carries a more powerful light and fog signal than the largest buoys in use, and is fully automatic.

Two light vessels and fourteen buoys served as wreck warning lights to mark the wrecks of the *Texaco Caribbean, Brandenberg* and *Nikki,* when they were involved in a multiple collision in the Dover Straits.

Trinity House, London, is now the General Lighthouse Authority for England, Wales, the Channel Islands and Gibraltar. It has the sole power of erecting lights for general navigation and is responsible for fixed and floating seamarks and visual, audible and electronic aids to navigation. Within its area of jurisdiction there are about 90 lighthouses, about 24 light vessels and nearly 700 buoys, over half of which are lighted. Where local and harbour authorities maintain seamarks within their own port limits they are regularly inspected by Trinity House. The sanction of the Corporation must be obtained before any changes can be made. Trinity House also has statutory powers over lights maintained by the General Lighthouse Authorities in Scotland and Ireland. Light dues, amounting annually to about £15,000,000, are levied at every port in the British Isles, and are used to finance the three General Lighthouse Authorities. These dues are based on the net registered tonnage of the vessel and are collected by Customs officers acting as agents.

Lighthouses not only mark dangerous rocks on headlands; they act as guides to approaching ships. Prior to lighthouses being built at Killingholme and Paull, in 1836, the Brethren at Hull Trinity House arranged for a light to be shown from a window in the Humber Tavern at Paull. The owner was paid two pounds a month for the rent of the room housing the lantern.

Once the lighthouses were built and put into service they proved to be of such assistance to pilots that others were eventually built at Thorngumbold and Salt End to enable the whole of the Lower Humber to be safely navigated. The lighthouses at Killingholme and Paull, however, were constantly under discussion because of the tidal drift and the hazardous sand banks. Not only was the high light at Killingholme raised by twenty feet, but new and improved French lamps were fitted in 1845, while six years later a further lighthouse was erected to the north of the existing one at Killingholme. From this new lighthouse a fixed white light was exhibited thirty-three feet above high water mark. Still later, in 1860, the high lighthouse, now standing 78 feet in height was painted red, while that to the south was white.

Another and more drastic change in the high lighthouse became necessary when it was struck by lightning which ripped away part of the dome over the lantern and caused considerable damage. Investigation showed that, quite apart from the storm damage, the deterioration of the stonework and base made it advisable to take down and rebuild the lighthouse and keeper's cottage completely.

View of Dungeness showing the two lighthouses before the construction of the nuclear power staions. Taken from the bridge of THPV *Penlee*.   *D. A. McDonald*

In 1536, when Newcastle Trinity House was founded, provision was made in the charter for the erection of a tower on each side of the mouth of the Tyne where the river narrows. These were built and in operation by 1540 and were equipped with lights so that ships could be guided into the river by night as well as by day. They were also intended to help defend the river in time of war. With only one tallow candle in each tower (later a second candle was added) they were very different from the lights we see streaming across the water from the lighthouses with which we are familiar today. English ships were charged a fee of twopence which was used for the upkeep of the lights; alien ships had to pay double that amount.

England's second lighthouse was at Tynemouth Castle where a coal fire was maintained in the tower. Several other attempts were made to establish lighthouses in different places but these efforts appear to have been unsuccessful until the seventeenth century when, following the powers granted to Trinity House of London by the 1594 Act the Brethren began to take an interest in these. With the growth of the coal trade, shipping between London and Newcastle was increasing, but without the aid of seamarks seamen preferred to keep close to the coast, thereby encountering dangerous shoals. Ship owners and masters of vessels using the route petitioned the authorities to provide seamarks, especially in the area of Lowestoft and Winterton. They were willing to pay one shilling per 100 tons towards the cost. Fishermen using that part of the coast were not so willing to pay and eventually were exempted from payment of dues and the charge was reduced to fourpence for other ships passing the light.

Lighthouses were built at Lowestoft and Caister, Trinity House receiving the fees paid by ships passing the lights. Lighting was limited to candles in the first instance and when lighting was improved there was trouble because the lighthouse keeper employed an old woman to do his job of attending the lights, and she failed to do so. As a result a new keeper was employed at a higher salary and the lighting was again improved.

There was a long and heated dispute before the first lighthouse at Dungeness was built and dues for its maintenance agreed, although the citizens of Rye claimed "that this light is needful to be maintained is proved for that the place is daungerous about it, that a shipp may be in 10 or 12 faddoms water and in a quarter of an houres sale may runne upon land, which would be an evitable danger to the night and dark weather . . . Besides experience showes that the steeple of Lyd, a towne neere by, doth unhappily present unto straungers uppon those seas the forme of a sale of some tall shipp which hath binn a meanes oftentimes towards night to incourage marriners to steere their course confidently that way, the rather because it is all low land neere the said steeple which seems as sea afarr off, whereby many shipps have suddenly out of their false supposition of this sea and saile and deepe sounding neere the land when night hath come on, runne on ground and perished, which dangerous mistake this light doth prevent."

Many reasons have been attributed to the authorities at Trinity House for their reluctance to build lighthouses until private individuals sought and sometimes obtained patents for these. One reason was obviously finance and the consequent charge imposed on shipping. Another was the false sense of security such aids might give to seamen, especially when the lights used were so primitive. Whatever may be true of the past, Trinity House has since adequately performed its duty to provide seamarks for the safety of shipping. Today a fleet of five lighthouse tenders relieve and supply light vessels and rock lighthouses, service buoys and locate and mark wrecks.

Lighthouses have been electrified and modern equipment installed, making a number of lighthouses fully automatic. One particular aid for mariners was the development of the Radar Beacon.

Trinity House having reported against a proposal for a light at Dungeness Point in 1600, now has one of the most modern, capable of automatic operation. It was the first of its kind to use the Xenon electric arc lamp as its source of illumination. All its main navigational aids are duplicated and are automatically changed to stand-by equipment in the event of failure. The whole of the tower is floodlit making it more readily seen by ships at sea. This has also had the effect of reducing the mortality rate of birds at this lighthouse during the migratory season.

The patent for the first lighthouse at Dungeness was granted to Sir Edward Howard in August 1615, and was the first British lighthouse erected solely for the benefit of general coastal navigation. Trinity House had withdrawn its opposition but when ship owners were angered by having to pay their dues to Customs officials, thus being unable to avoid payment, they joined forces with Trinity House in an endeavour to suppress the lighthouse. They claimed that it was a nuisance to navigation because of its poor light which relied on candles instead of the coal fire originally used for light. Seamen also complained of the distance of the lighthouse from the sea and in 1635 a tower was built nearer the Point with a coal fire on top.

Again there were disputes about poor lighting and Trinity House insisted that better

Cherokee sets a 100-ton buoy on the waves off Virginia Beach.

U.S. Coast Guard

illumination must be provided. The next complaint came in 1746 not, in this instance on account of poor illumination, although a coal fire was still the source of light, but because the sea had receded which left the tower a long way from the water's edge and in consequence the light was misleading.

Nothing appears to have been done about this until 1792 when a tower 116 feet high was built. It was lit by 18 sperm-oil lamps. This served for over a hundred years in spite of the fact that, during the nineteenth century, lightning struck the tower making a rent in the masonry on the north side.

In 1862 an electric light was installed making Dungeness lighthouse the first in England to be illuminated by this means. It was also made more conspicuous in daylight by painting the tower black with a white band.

At the beginning of the nineteenth century yet another new lighthouse was built at Dungeness, the continued recession of the sea making this necessary. This had a comparatively short life because a Nuclear Power Station had been erected nearby which obscured the navigational light, hence the extremely modern and efficient lighthouse of today.

A beacon was first erected on Wolf Rock, near Land's End, in 1791, but the sea soon carried it away. Another beacon, which took five years to build, was completed successfully in 1840. About twenty years later work commenced on a granite tower which took eight years to complete. The tower shows a white red alternating flash every thirty seconds and is visible for 16.4 miles in clear weather. It has a diaphone signal giving one report every thirty seconds.

The Royal Sovereign Lighthouse, situated six miles off Eastbourne, was commissioned in 1971 and has a helicopter landing deck. Its light is exhibited 112 feet above sea level and has a range of 28 miles to the horizon. Further aids include a radio beacon and a signal with a range of four to five miles.

Eddystone lighthouse is probably the most famous, being the first lighthouse to be built on a small rock in the open sea. It was built of wood and completed in 1698. Winstanley, its designer, was so confident of its strength to withstand the force of wind and sea that he said he would like to be occupying it during a gale. His wish was, unfortunately, granted for while spending several days effecting some repairs, one of the worst recorded storms arose and the next morning both the lighthouse, its designer and all his men had disappeared. The lighthouse had been in use for only five years.

The next was built of oak and iron and stood for forty-seven years when it was completely destroyed by fire after burning for five days. As a temporary measure to guard the position, a light vessel was substituted. Smeaton was the next designer and work commenced in 1756. It was the first stone lighthouse to be built in the open sea and it stood for one hundred and twenty years. Smeaton—a clockmaker—went to enormous trouble to give it the necessary strength to withstand the elements. The principal keeper recorded that, during the first big storm "the house did shake as if a man had been in a great tree" and the men were "almost frightened out of their lives." He added, "the fear seized them in the back but rubbing them with oil of turpentine gave them relief." Rock lighthouses still

Large Navigational Buoy which replaced lightship on the East Coast, U.S.A.   *U.S. Coast Guard*

shake in violent storms, with pictures sometimes being thrown off the walls, but the men are no longer "frightened out of their lives."

Smeaton's lighthouse was first lit by 24 candles. These were replaced, after fifty years, by 24 oil lamps with reflectors behind them until, in 1845, a refracting lens with a single light in the centre was installed.

The present granite lighthouse was built in 1878 on a nearby rock and opened in 1882. Larger stones were used and Smeaton's model was improved upon. The light is now 140 feet above water, the previous one being only 96 feet. The stump of Smeaton's tower can still be seen on the original rock.

Both American and Canadian seamarks come under the jurisdiction of their respective Coast Guard services. Of the 45,000 aids to navigation under the jurisdiction of the United States Coast Guard over half are buoys which are serviced by buoy tenders. Some of these tenders are equipped with an ice-breaking bow. Included in these 45,000 aids are nearly 400 lighthouses and more than 13,000 minor lights situated in or near prominent coastal points, channels and their entrances, lakes, waterways and dangerous rocks, reefs and shoals. Most of the 50 lightships have been replaced by offshore towers or large navigational buoys. The Columbia lightship, one of the few remaining in active duty, has a radio beacon synchronised with a two-tone fog signal which broadcasts to ships using it as an aid to navigation.

Ships from many parts of the world pass in view of the tower of the Ambrose Offshore Light Structure which replaced the Ambrose Lightship at the lower bay entrance to New York Harbour seven miles west of Sandy Hook, New Jersey.

The Canadian Coast Guard maintains and supplies shore-based and floating aids in Canadian waters, on rivers, the Great Lakes and other inland waters. As in America, ice-breaking is important and nine full ice-breaking ships are in use and an equal number of lighthouses and buoy tenders. These give primary ice-breaking support to shipping in Arctic areas.

Perhaps one of the greatest aids to navigation is radar. Many ports have modern radar stations either under the control of harbour authorities or of the pilots themselves. These give round the clock navigational service and are especially valuable in foggy or hazy weather and for guiding ships sailing in narrow channels. Liverpool was the first major port in the world to establish a shore-based radar service linked by radio to the ships using the port to aid their safe navigation within the harbour. The Harbour Surveillance Radar in operation at Tees Dock since 1967 provides shore-based precision coverage of the entire estuary and its approaches, permitting positive control of all ships fitted with V.H.F. radio.

The primary function of the Harbour Surveillance Radar at Milford Haven is to provide vessels with information to enable them to take the necessary steps to ensure that they do not meet in congested parts of the Haven or at West Angle buoy or the entrance. In the event of vessels entering or leaving the port and suddenly becoming affected by fog, special information is passed to them.

Radar Station, Europort.   *Royal Netherlands Navy*

P (477)
(L District)

No. 2375

To all to whom these Presents shall come, The Corporation of Trinity House of Deptford Strond, send Greeting, **know ye** that in pursuance and by virtue of the powers given them for that purpose in and by The Pilotage Act 1913, and of all other powers them enabling, the said Corporation, having first duly examined *DEREK RAYMOND GODFREY* of *3, GEORGE V AVENUE, WESTBROOK, MARGATE, KENT,* : **Mariner,** (the Bearer hereof, whose description is endorsed on these Presents) and having, upon such examination, found the said *DEREK RAYMOND GODFREY* to be a fit and competent Person, duly skilled to act as a Pilot for the purpose of conducting Ships, sailing, navigating, and passing within the limits hereinafter mentioned, **Do** hereby appoint and license the said *DEREK RAYMOND GODFREY* to act as a Pilot, for the purpose of conducting Ships from *DUNGENESS THROUGH THE SOUTH CHANNELS UP THE RIVER THAMES TO GRAVESEND AND UP THE RIVER MEDWAY TO STANGATE CREEK AND ALSO (BUT ONLY IN CASE OF EMERGENCY OR WITH THE EXPRESS SANCTION IN EACH CASE OF THE TRINITY HOUSE) VICE VERSA, INTO AND OUT OF FOLKESTONE, DOVER, RAMSGATE AND MARGATE HARBOURS, ALSO FROM THE HARBOURS OF FOLKESTONE, DOVER, RAMSGATE AND MARGATE TO DUNGENESS.*

And this Licence (if the same shall not be revoked or suspended in the meantime, as in the said Act provided), is to continue in force up to and until the 31st day of January next ensuing the date of these Presents, but no longer, unless renewed from time to time by Indorsement hereon. Provided always that the said Pilot shall so long comply with all the Bye-laws and Regulations made or to be made by the said Corporation.

This Licence shall not authorise or empower the said *DEREK RAYMOND GODFREY* to take charge as a Pilot of any Ship or Vessel drawing more than *SIXTEEN* **Feet Water** (except when an upper draught Pilot is not available to offer his services), in the Rivers Thames or Medway or any of the Channels leading thereto or therefrom, until it shall be certified hereon that the said *DEREK RAYMOND GODFREY* has acted as a Licensed Pilot for three Years, and has been on re-examination approved of in that behalf by the said Corporation.

Given under the Common Seal of the Corporation of Trinity House of Deptford Strond, this *TENTH* day of *FEBRUARY* 19*59*.

Deputy Master.

J. W. Burleigh
Secretary.

CHAPTER SIX

Role and Qualifications of Pilots

IN 1911, before the United Kingdom Pilotage Act of 1913 was promulgated allowing exemption from compulsory pilotage to certain vessels, a report was issued in which it was stated:

"To prevent risks being improperly run, and to induce the maintenance of an adequate service of pilots, it is both in the interest of the State and of shipowners, masters, pilots and others, that pilotage should be made compulsory in every port where a pilotage system is reasonably necessary."

In spite of this report, under the Act exemptions from compulsory pilotage were granted to ships regardless of the qualifications of those masters or mates who manned the vessel, and irrespective of how infrequently they used that particular port. Pilotage certificates were even renewed after the master had retired.

There has always been a great deal of discussion concerning the necessity or otherwise for pilots to bring ships into and out of ports. The result is that compulsory pilotage has been the practice in some districts, with certain exceptions, and not in others. Some ship owners are reluctant to pay pilotage fees, and some masters do not like relinquishing control of their ship. Anomalies exist in different parts of the country. For example, Tees Pilotage Authority estimate that about eighty per cent of the vessels navigating in their area use the pilotage service, in spite of the fact that it is still a voluntary district because of the refusal of an application made in 1962 for compulsory pilotage to be legalised. The high percentage of vessels using pilots in this case is probably due to the dangerous nature of the cargo carried.

Where pilotage certificates are issued to masters or mates they are usually required to pass examinations, to undertake a certain number of voyages to the port in question, and to undergo a medical examination. The facility of allowing masters holding certificates to pilot their own vessels has been extended, in some countries, to permit them to pilot other vessels.

All Trinity House districts, even the smallest, are compulsory, but with high tonnage exemption limits. In all districts where compulsory pilotage does apply there are a number of exemptions depending on the tonnage of the vessel and whether masters of ships constantly using a particular port have been able to claim such exemption. This explains why only about fifty per cent of vessels in the London district have a licensed pilot on board. In any case, the Pilotage Act, as it stands at present, prevents compulsory pilotage applying in closed docks and locks. This affects shipping in Manchester Ship Canal where highly skilled navigation is essential in such confined waters. Another anomaly is that ships passing through a district en route for another port do not require a pilot, although conditions are the same as if they were entering the port.

Pilot's Licence.
Trinity House

The Steering Committee on Pilotage, set up in September, 1973, found that the European situation is different, inasmuch as in France and Holland pilotage dues are paid whether or not a pilot is taken, while in Germany a basic charge is applied to all ships, with an additional charge when a pilot is engaged. The effect of this is that the great majority of vessels take pilots although only those vessels in France and Holland carrying dangerous goods are under compulsion to do so; while in Germany compulsory pilotage is limited to certain areas. In Italy it is compulsory.

In America most of the business community and marine insurance companies were active in their support of compulsory pilotage, opposition coming mainly from tug and barge interests in New England who wished to avoid paying pilotage fees. The struggle for stability for American pilotage went on from 1886, with the emergence of a national programme, until 1917, when America entered the First World War, at which time anti-pilotage forces were overridden and the original law of 1789 was sustained.

In South Australia compulsory pilotage was first introduced in March 1838 at Port Adelaide. Subsequently other ports began to develop and compulsory pilotage was progressively introduced at different ports.

Pilotage is compulsory in 16 ports in New Zealand unless the master is regularly trading to that port and holds a special exemption, or the vessel is under 100 tons, but amendments to the Harbours Act of 1950 which may affect those regulations relating to pilot exemption certificates, are under consideration at present.

In Tasmania all ships are required to employ a pilot but the masters of certain vessels trading around the Australian coast and on the Inter-Commonwealth trade between New Zealand and Australia, may be exempted after they have made three voyages into and from Hobart in charge of a pilot. In such cases the master may be examined in his knowledge of the port and, if successful, he is permitted to navigate within the port area without the services of a pilot, provided that the vessel, irrespective of type, does not exceed 500 feet in length and also provided that the vessel, no matter what the length, is not carrying or is not capable of carrying inflammable liquid or dangerous cargo in bulk.

With regard to compulsory pilotage in the United Kingdom, the Steering Committee recommended changes in the 1913 Pilotage Act to make pilotage compulsory as a general principle subject to carefully considered local exemptions. These recommendations are given in more detail in the Policy Statement on Marine Pilotage Rec. 8 (see Appendix A). Since these Recommendations have not yet been included in the legislative programme before Parliament, a resolution was passed by the U.K. Pilots' Association at their Annual Conference in November 1975 that:—

(a) in the interests of safety the association urge Pilotage Authorities to introduce and/or extend compulsory pilotage in their pilotage districts; and

(b) in the event of a Pilotage Authority declining to do so, the U.K.P.A. will promote a Pilotage Order on behalf of the majority of licensed Pilots of the District to give effect to the above.

In proposing the resolution Mr G. A. Coates (Tees and Executive Member) said "It would bring order and greater safety to many of our ports. The lack of compulsory pilotage in

1975 in many of our large commercial, industrial ports is a nuisance that should be ended."

One of the reasons why the piloting of ships into and out of ports became compulsory in many places was because pilots, with their years of seafaring experience, daily contact, constant observation, practical skill and special training for the task, are thoroughly familiar with their own localities. They know if the channels change, if a storm carries away a buoy or extinguishes a light, or if a wreck is obstructing the channel. They are thus the best men to bring ships safely into and out of port. Shipmasters who are away from the harbours for long periods, or are constantly using different ports, are not always aware of these things. In fact, pilotage has rightly been defined as "the temporary engagement of a specialist."

A further resolution passed at the U.K.P.A. Annual Conference in November 1975 concerned the payment of pilotage dues by shipowners whose masters have been granted a pilotage certificate. The resolution was proposed by Mr D. I. McMillan (London River pilot and Vice-President) with the unanimous agreement of the Executive.

Many pilots have lived in an atmosphere of harbours and ships all their lives, as their fathers and other members of the family have done. Mr Mackenzie, a retired Clyde pilot, says:

"I was a shipmaster for seven years and then I was a Clyde pilot for more than thirty years. My grandfather was a shipowner and my father and my many uncles commanded his ships. My own everyday life was lived in an atmosphere of harbours and ships in which the only people with any real existence were harbour workers, seamen and pilots. I took it for granted that when I grew up I should go to sea with a view to becoming, ultimately, a harbour master or a pilot. I became a Clyde pilot. Before I did so I served in ships of almost every kind—tugs, dredgers, puffers, schooners, jiggers, coasters and deep sea ships. Everywhere I went I drew plans of the harbours, plans which later became very useful to me when I took out a certificate as being competent to pilot ships round all the coasts of Britain."

This family connection with the sea, and pilotage in particular, is repeated over and over again at many different ports. "Dido" Bradford, a retired Exmouth pilot, whose portrait is on the sign displayed over the *Pilot Inn* by the docks, was for thirty-one years in the service of Trinity House, while his brother, Percy, served for forty-one years.

Until 1939 there was hardly a road in Northfleet or Gravesend which did not have some connection with the river. The build-up of ships' disasters resulted in pilotage being made compulsory here.

With a few exceptions conditions for obtaining a pilot's licence for a large port are similar for all countries, the main requirement being a master's or first officer's foreign-going certificate with a specified period of sea service. Most countries also require a medical examination on entry and at regular intervals thereafter.

In some countries pilots are employed by the State, in others they are self-employed, as in the United Kingdom. Whichever method applies pilots of the same class earn approximately the same amount.

The U.K. Steering Committee found that training schedules in each country are

London River Pilots waiting for ships to arrive. Their room is surrounded with charts.

Sport and General Press Agency

roughly similar, "with examinations taken before or after appointments, or sometimes both, together with practical training through accompanying experienced pilots on pilotage duties. In all cases newly licensed pilots are restricted for a number of years to piloting vessels of limited size."

The majority of United Kingdom pilots are recruited by local pilotage authorities mainly from the merchant service. Requirements vary slightly in different districts but nearly all insist on British nationality and a high standard of medical fitness.

Variations dictated by the bye-laws of the districts in the United Kingdom sometimes inhibit transfers of pilots from one area to another. For example, Clyde Pilotage Authority recruits men who have held command of a vessel or served as chief officer and held a master's foreign-going certificate of competency. Trinity House London not only requires such a certificate for the larger districts, and stipulates that candidates must be under thirty-five years of age, but that they must also have had eight years experience in charge of a watch.

To achieve a Master's Foreign-Going Certificate it is necessary to serve a deep sea apprenticeship which, in the case of most serving pilots, was four years commencing between the ages of fifteen and a half and seventeen and a half. Today's apprentices are all nearer seventeen owing to the present requirement of three GCE 'O' levels. At the end of this time, and usually after further training, they take a Second Mate's F.G. Certificate. This entitles them to serve up to the rank of second mate on a deep sea vessel. Then they must return to sea in order to qualify for the first mate's F.G. Certificate, and after yet another two years at sea they can qualify for the Master's F.G. Certificate. Most men spend at least three months intensive training prior to examinations to qualify for certificates; failure can result in a return to sea for a period up to six months before being allowed to sit the examination again.

A large proportion of pilots working from Gravesend, especially river pilots, have either been masters of vessels regularly trading into London, or pilots elsewhere. After completing their eight years deep sea watch keeping service, as required by Trinity House, candidates are interviewed by the London Pilotage Committee which includes two ship-owners, three Elder Brethren, one Port of London Authority representative and two pilots. If successful they will either be listed for sea pilotage, which combines Channel Inwards (North) and Inwards (South) handling ships below Gravesend to and from the limits of the London district, or for river pilotage, which is the area from Gravesend to London Bridge, or for the River Medway, where pilots work both on that river and to seaward limits of the district. There may then be a wait of as much as two years before a vacancy occurs, and even when "called" they must "trip" with other pilots for a period of three to six months, during which time they receive no remuneration and must stamp their own insurance cards. To pass the medical examination they must have excellent health, eyesight and hearing. This is essential because a pilot has to stand on the bridge for many hours on end, in all weathers, at all hours of the day and night and still retain his concentration.

Manchester Ship Canal has a scheme of entry and training whereby candidates must serve four years as a helmsman on the canal before they can take the qualifying examination for a pilot's licence. Helmsmen are normally recruited at the age of twenty-seven or twenty-eight and must have a master's foreign-going certificate. They are self-employed and receive no pay for the first month or six weeks and in most respects are organised exactly as the pilots, their eventual earnings being pooled. These men develop their techniques to a very high level. They actually steer the ship under licence from the Canal Company, taking moral responsibility, though the pilot corrects any tendency to error. Helmsmen hold their permits from the Port Authority and have, for technical reasons, never come directly under the jurisdiction of the Pilotage Committee. They have separate representation at meetings with the Authority and, in practice, attend many of the meetings with pilots' representatives. Roughly one-third of piloted ships require the services of a helmsman, of whom there are about thirty.

Some districts in the United Kingdom, such as those on the East Coast, the Bristol Channel area and Liverpool, have apprenticeship schemes. In Liverpool pilots are trained from boyhood in the Service so that eventually they can take the responsibility of piloting the largest ships in the world. Licensed pilots in Liverpool are recruited from these apprentice pilots who serve much of their apprenticeship on board the pilot boats. Applicants must be sixteen years or over and hold four 'O' level GCE passes. They are given a two-week induction course at a technical college before serving as cadets on a foreign-going ship for six months. Apprenticeship to the pilotage service follows and covers a period of seven years during which time they serve as boathands on pilot boats and on river launches learning about tides, lights, depths, signals and the seamanship required over the whole area of the Liverpool Pilotage District. They can progress from junior boathand through different grades until, towards the end of their apprenticeship, they become senior boathands when they must obtain their certificate of competency as second mates. If they satisfy the Examination Committee they can then be licensed as third class pilots, restricted to ships of up to 600 tons net. When their apprenticeship is successfully completed and they have served as second class and then first class pilots they can do leadsman's duties on ships of the 200,000 ton class over a period of five years, by which time they become senior first class pilots, able to pilot ships of any tonnage.

When apprenticeship started in Hull boys of twelve years went to sea while waiting to be appointed. In recent years they came in at sixteen and served a five-year apprenticeship, dividing the time between study at school, serving on the pilot cutter and accompanying pilots on duty. Pilot-apprenticeships have, however, now been discontinued.

A record of the articles of apprenticeship in America, dated 1801, states that John Kelso, a lad of sixteen years, "voluntarily and of his own free will and accord put himself apprentice to John Funck of the City of New York." Apprenticeship was for a period of five years and the articles reveal the rigid restrictions of the time:—

". . . the said apprentice his master faithfully shall serve, his secrets keep, his lawful commands everywhere readily obey; he shall do no damage to his master, nor see it done by others without letting or giving notice thereof to his master . . . he shall not commit matrimony within the said term and at cards, dice or any unlawful game he shall not play, whereby his master shall have damage, with his own goods, nor the goods of others, without licence from his said master. He shall neither buy nor sell; he shall not absent himself day or night from his master's service without leave, nor haunt ale houses, taverns or playhouses; but in all things shall behave himself as a faithful apprentice ought to do, within the said term. And said master shall use the utmost of his endeavour to teach or cause to be taught or instructed the said apprentice in the trade and mystery of a pilot for the piloting of vessels to and from the City of New York, by Sandy Hooke, and during the same term of five years shall pay to said apprentice the sum of seven dollars per month until the said apprentice shall be appointed boatkeeper, after which he shall pay him the wages usually allowed to boatkeepers."

There are still restrictions on drinking while on duty and severe penalties should a man be found to be drunk while piloting, and although many of the more rigid social restrictions have changed with the passage of time, proficiency and a high social code of conduct is an essential requirement for all pilots.

Trouble arises when masters of ships are not subject to severe penalties for being drunk when sailing in non-compulsory waters. Recently such a master was fined a mere £50 with £25 costs for drinking in his bunk while the mate at the wheel, young and inexperienced, steered the vessel in such a manner that it was described as "meandering drunkenly up the Thames." The police boarded the ship after its erratic course had been observed on radar. The crew, with the exception of the master and mate, were Portuguese, while the vessel, operating from Exmouth, was registered in Panama.

Most States in America have an apprenticeship scheme. Where this is not so, masters or chief mates of ocean going vessels who hold federal pilots licences for particular areas undergo a period of training and must demonstrate their competency as pilots. Apprentices are graded as juniors and seniors, and those in New York must be citizens of U.S.A. and not less than eighteen years of age. They must hold a certificate of graduation from a secondary school, or a licence as a deck officer for vessels of 500 tons or over; be physically and mentally sound; have normal eyesight and hearing; be free of speech impediment, and be of good character and temperament "suited to meet the demands of the pilot service." Part of their training during the first four years is devoted to practical instruction on inward and outward-bound vessels and the method of handling them. They are acquainted with steering apparatus, the engine room, signals, compass and other navigational aids on the vessel. They also receive instruction on tides, currents, soundings, bearings, distances of shoals, rocks, bars, points of land, buoys, beacons and lights. They have to become familiar with charts and tide tables, as well as with records of the United States Weather Bureau. Each apprentice must make at least 150 trips with a pilot either inward or outward before he can obtain a licence. After two years he may apply for a position as boatkeeper. In the past this meant that he was eligible to captain a sailing pilot vessel. Today he is eligible as a mate or captain on a modern pilot vessel.

The U.K. Steering Committee, as a result of their investigations, recommended that "direct entry from the merchant service should be adopted as the standard for the future," and that "a certificate of competency as master foreign-going, or its equivalent, should normally be the minimum qualification although it is recognised that, in certain ports, a lower grade of certificate would be allowed." They add that "existing apprenticeship

Apprentices working Liverpool pilot boat at Liverpool Bar. *Mersey Docks and Harbour Board, Liverpool*

schemes would need to be phased out but obligations to apprentices now undergoing training should be fulfilled." Pilots at some of the ports will doubtless raise a certain amount of opposition to the phasing out of apprenticeship schemes, especially those who have entered the service in that way, but in spite of this, the Steering Committee found, during its visits to the ports, that "there was a general awareness that a common qualification and method of entry could be to the advantage of all."

In the London district, having accompanied fully qualified pilots for three to six months, candidates are examined by an Examination Panel of Trinity House before being issued with a licence as an underdraught, or junior pilot. This licence is renewed each year after the pilot has satisfied an Elder Brother that he is conversant with changes in his district, and provided that his eyesight and physical fitness continue to be satisfactory. It is interesting to note that the licence is still printed on parchment and has to be sprinkled with powder before it can be renewed.

Pilots are graded according to experience and ability, with variations in different districts largely governed by the size and type of shipping using the port. For example, in the London district the following class restrictions are in operation:—

	CHANNEL	CINQUE PORTS	NORTH CHANNEL	RIVER MEDWAY
4th Class	2,000 G.R.T. 2 years	2,000 G.R.T. 2 years	—	16 FEET DRAUGHT and 3,500 G.R.T. 2 years
3rd Class	6,000 G.R.T. 1 year	4,500 G.R.T. 1 year	14 FEET DRAUGHT and 12,000 G.R.T. 3 years	3,500 G.R.T. 1 year
2nd Class	12,000 G.R.T. 1 year	12,000 G.R.T. 1 year	12,000 G.R.T. 1 year	17,500 G.R.T. 1 year
1st Class	NIL	NIL	NIL	NIL

All London pilots in the major branches have now become first class for those who retire are not being replaced because of the fall in shipping. Among the London pilots there are a number of Choice pilots.

Mr H. M. Hignett, Manchester Ship Canal pilot, in his report on his tour of overseas ports, writes:—

"In none of the ports visited were there appropriated (or choice) pilots; those pilots selected by the shipowner to pilot his vessels when moving in the district. Nor did I find any pilot or pilot association which thought that they were useful or necessary. In about three ports there were systems using a group of senior pilots for V.L.C.C.'s. In Rotterdam the qualification was that of age; pilots with at least ten years service and between the ages of forty-five and fifty-five were the persons to pilot the super-tankers in Europort. A similar custom operates in certain of the Thames districts."

This system of Choice pilots applies to passenger ships and container ships in particular. Some districts, such as Liverpool, use the term "Appropriated Pilots" for this

Outward Pilots (Channel) en route for Dungeness and Gravesend. *D. A. McDonald*

class, while in the Clyde district they are known as "Selected" or "Appropriated." Choice pilots are firmly established in Southampton. This use of a special class of pilot has caused considerable discontent among pilots in some of the ports who would like to see it discontinued. However, in general shipowners approve of the system. There are no Choice pilots in the Netherlands, Germany or France.

In addition to having first, second and third class pilots, the Humber pilotage authority decided that, after a pilot had operated for six years in the first class, he could become a Senior First Class Pilot qualified to handle large tankers and bulk carriers.

Milford Haven has four classes of pilots, but no Choice pilots. Following the usual entry conditions of holding a Master's certificate and accompanying pilots for the first three to six months, the men sit for fourth class licence which enables them to take ships up to 10,000 tons for the first twelve months when they can qualify for third class and, if successful, take ships up to 30,000 tons. Following this they can become second class and take ships up to 50,000 tons, while after a further twelve months they are licensed to take the largest of the V.L.C.C.'s which may range from 150,000 to 320,000 tons dead weight.

The Inwards South pilots who work from Folkestone also have four grades, each taking ships of varying tonnage. In addition they have Middle Cut and Inner List pilots who take large oil tankers. There are Choice pilots here but they are gradually being phased out.

Rotterdam, which claims to be the largest port in the world, also claims that no other port in the world has organised pilot training as they have. All Rotterdam pilots are salaried and they are constantly recruiting men who come into the service at twenty-seven to thirty years of age as apprentices after ten years seagoing experience, by which time they have a certificate as master mariner. This does not mean, however, that they have been handling ships as masters. Anyone below the rank of master, sometimes even his first officer, seldom has manoeuvring experience of handling a vessel. This tends to limit his sense of responsibility. All prospective pilots come in on the apprenticeship scheme having undergone a psychological and aptitude test. Following a six week course in the town "Den Helder" and one on the pilot cutter, they have to attend a class in the pilots' office on one day a week. During this period of their training they make two hundred trips on the river with big and small ships, with different pilots. After undergoing an examination they make ten trips under the supervision of pilots before qualifying for a licence.

There are some men, known as Deep Sea pilots, who hold Deep Sea Certificates issued by the London, Newcastle and Hull Trinity Houses and by Clyde Pilotage Authority, who work generally through commercial agencies in waters beyond any pilotage district. Their services are increasingly in demand.

Rotterdam pilotage authority have built a simulator of a completely new line-mock-up of fairway or river unit. They have also built a mock-up of a ship's bridge showing the movement of ships. This gives a means of standardised training in a short amount of time.

The U.K. Steering Committee recommended that there should be a nationally agreed training programme for their United Kingdom pilots, probably including simulator training.

Pilots in Hull area attend Hull Nautical College where simulated courses for pilots are thought to have been the most successful of all those held at this College. Two general purpose computers are used to provide dynamical simulation of many of the navigational aids used at sea, and comprehensive training is given in their use.

For the Pilotage and Shore Surveillance Simulator Course exercises, a sixteen inch Decca radar display is used in conjunction with V.H.F. and a computer teletype which prints out positions of ships in the area on demand. The course includes, among other things, manoeuvring and collision avoidance exercises in pilotage waters, the problems particular to large vessels in narrow waters, position fixing by radar, the function of the shore station in distress and emergencies, and demonstrations of actual collision cases.

A one-week elementary radar simulator course is held in a room containing three cubicles equipped with radar, one having helm and speed controls. Five targets are available on this simulator in addition to various land effects.

The advanced radar and navigational aid simulator course covers collision avoidance by radar, emphasis being placed upon the particular problems caused by crowded shipping areas, narrow channels and vessels not complying with recommended routeing. The simulator can display the Straits of Dover with a total of fifty-one vessels moving at any one time. Research is carried out into the reactions of navigators in heavy traffic and their ability to assess immediate and potential hazards. Shiphandling provides an appreciation of the capabilities and limitations of different types of vessel when manoeuvring in open or confined waters. The co-ordinated use of navigational aids is demonstrated by an exercise showing the dangers involved in relying exclusively upon one aid, and evaluating and comparing the information obtained from different aids; the use of correction tables; catering for human errors and blunders and coping with complete instrument failure. Finally, this course covers bridge organisation with exercises in making the most effective

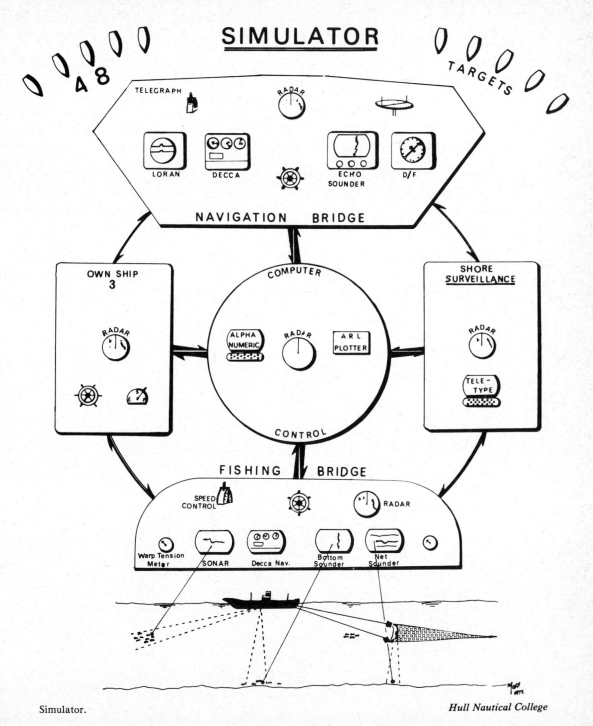

Simulator.

use of the personnel available for efficient watchkeeping during reduced visibility, consideration being given to the problems of fatigue and the layout of equipment. The use of general purpose computers on board ships is a growing trend and the digital computer has been used effectively to produce land echoes.

This type of training is much favoured in some places, while in others it is considered that simulators are not the best means of training pilots because they can give no sense of responsibility. If anything goes wrong it is the pilot's pride that is hurt, not the ship.

In a report on the Education and Training of Maritime Pilots, presented at the end of the Liverpool Seminar held in April, 1972, Mr C. A. Rhodes, Medway pilot, having stressed the importance of education, said that "although a simulator might well provide useful preliminary guidance on the behaviour and characteristics of standard vessels in textbook situations; might also give some indication of the effect of wind, tide and auxiliary power, such as tugs and thrusters, of the effects upon manoeuvrability from minimal under-keel clearances and changing channel contours; it can be no real substitute for the practical experience of ship handling in real life situations. Even the most sophisticated simulator won't bring out the sweat beads, set the adrenalin racing through the system, or have the pilot turning the ship through his own physical exertion on the bridge dodgers (wind deflectors) . . . Only when you are on your own on a dirty night for the first time, when there is no one to turn to for help or advice, and when any mistake is going to cost real money or even real lives, only then do you realise what it is all about. Then the training really starts. There is the essence of training and for the practical part of a pilot's work there really can be no alternative but practice and experience."

Radar was a luxury twenty-five years ago, most senior pilots having had to learn the hard way. Navigation was done largely by bearing and distance off a known point with a chart to consult and a margin for error. Now Radar Observer Certificates are required as an integral part of all certificates for Masters or Mates.

In countries other than the United Kingdom and the New York/New Jersey Pilots little attempt has been made towards further education of pilots after their initial licence has been granted. Facilities for radar training, which are available in most ports, do not appear to be used by pilots.

In the United Kingdom, apart from the Trinity House districts, each district has its own pilotage authority which is responsible for making its own bye-laws which have to be approved by the Department of Trade, under whose jurisdiction pilotage is officially placed. (See Appendix B for authorities in the United Kingdom.) All Trinity House outports have sub-commissioners who form a committee normally composed of representatives of the Harbour Authority, shipowners using the port, pilots and men with nautical experience. Other districts have similarly composed committees operating under their respective authorities.

As shown in Appendix B there are about forty pilotage authorities operating in the United Kingdom, Trinity House London being the largest: (see Appendix C). One of the recommendations of the Steering Committee is that a Central Pilotage Board should be established to be composed of people with first-hand experience of pilotage services.

Some of the matters which it recommended should come under the jurisdiction of such a Central Board would be:—

(a) Recruitment and training:

formulating recruitment qualifications, aptitude testing arrangements and training applicable to pilotage generally, but leaving actual recruitment, local training and testing to pilotage authorities.

(b) Transfers between pilotage districts:

adopting minimum entry standards which would assist mobility, proposing transfers where work load justifies this, and maintaining a list of candidates for transfer.

(c) Terms and conditions of service:

(d) Disciplinary appeals and surveillance of inquiries:

(e) Pilotage charges, accounting methods and contingency fund:

(f) Surveillance of and criteria for the proper number of pilots:

(g) Statistics, research and manpower planning:

(h) Pilot cutters and launches:

exercising an overall surveillance of the availability and condition of pilot boats, the prospective capital commitment for replacements and facilitating provision of finance to meet such commitments.

(i) Orders, byelaws and regulations:

originating orders, byelaws and regulations for the service, vetting those originated by pilotage authorities, and giving general advice on their coverage and drafting.

The Board would also be concerned with other, more general administrative matters.

Pilots in the United Kingdom, as in France and the Federal Republic of W. Germany, are self-employed, but in Holland they are salaried, sea pilots being civil servants under the Dutch Ministry of Defence, while harbour pilots are employed by the City of Rotterdam. There has been considerable discussion among pilots in the United Kingdom concerning this matter, but while some have been in favour of a salaried status, the large majority prefer to retain their independent position of self-employment and continue to pool their earnings. The Steering Committee discussed the issue with consultants appointed by the Conciliation and Advisory Service, as a result of which they have recommended that the present system be retained. The consultants felt that the "spirit of independent self-reliance of the successful would inevitably be at odds with the constraints of salaried employment . . ." They took the view that "the task of setting up and making effective a central body, which they favoured, would be difficult enough without the additional complication of introducing a salaried structure which would be strongly resisted by the majority of pilots at a time when their maximum co-operation should be sought." They did recommend, however, that "some central machinery should be established to secure uniform and equitable application of the remuneration system and related work indices as between different ports, and that pilots should contribute from their gross earnings towards a fund it was proposed to be set up to compensate for loss of earnings in the short term due to causes outside pilots' control."

Self-employment is favoured by pilots as being the best incentive to give them a sense

Rotterdam harbour pilot station, Merwehaven.   *Royal Netherlands Navy*

of responsibility to perform acts of pilotage whatever the time of day or the state of the weather.

For many years most pilots have pooled the fees they have obtained from acts of pilotage, while shipping or landing money is paid for the upkeep of the launch and launch crews' wages.

Trinity House pilots collect their own fees and the balance, after deduction of the amount due to pilots, is sent to Trinity House for the pension fund, 15 per cent, and administration, 4 per cent.

The measure of payment for pilotage is generally based on the footage of draught, or the registered gross or net tonnage of the vessel, and occasionally with all three. Additional charges are made in some cases for special pilotage services in port, for detaining a pilot and always when a pilot is carried to sea against his will.

Pilotage authorities do not all prescribe uniform, but as long ago as January, 1852 Hull Trinity House, at the request of their pilots, adopted a uniform suit "in order to distinguish them when on duty." It was officially agreed that commodores should wear a single breasted blue coat with nine buttons on the front and three on the cuffs, while pilots should wear a double breasted blue jacket with the same distinguishing buttons omitting those on the cuffs, the masters of each pilot cutter to wear a double breasted blue coat with three buttons on the cuffs.

In all countries a strict code of discipline is imposed. Pilots may be suspended from duty or have their licences revoked for negligence, incapacity, intoxication while on duty, refusal to take charge of a vessel without a satisfactory reason when requested, leaving a vessel without consent of the master and before their services have been fully and completely performed, and for grounding a vessel, or for being in collision.

In the past discipline was unnecessarily strict—even unjust—as when a pilot was directed by the Cardiff dockmaster to take a ship to sea to ease the congestion in the docks. Knowing that there was insufficient water to do this, the pilot refused to sail the ship, as a result of which his licence was suspended for twelve months for "failure to obey the directions of the dockmaster." A pilot had been suspended previously for a similar reason and both cases aroused considerable indignation, while Commander Cawley, later to become first President of the U.K. Pilots' Association, was so disapproving of the injustice of the pilotage ban that he resigned his position as pilot master of Cardiff. At that time pilots were not represented on any committee of the Pilotage Authority and had no means of appeal against any action which might be taken against them.

In the latter half of the nineteenth century there was considerable discontent among pilots. Remuneration was so poor that one pilot wrote to Hull Trinity House saying that as the trade did not support the present number of pilots he was resigning in order to earn a living by keeping a small shop. At that time the average annual earning per pilot was £55. 9s. 5½d. from which he had to pay about one pound per month expenses.

Many grievances were caused by the fact that the pilots thought too many masters held licences to pilot their own vessels, thus causing depreciation of the pilotage service by considerably reducing the work load and resulting remuneration of the regular pilots. The situation was further aggravated by the granting of certificates to aliens. Objections to this were raised by the pilots partly because it was considered a national danger to give a great many foreigners intimate and practical knowledge of the approaches to harbours and ports, and also because it depleted the limited income of British pilots. Even a small number of aliens holding certificates may greatly affect the receipts of pilots of a port or district.

In 1882 the Commissioners of the Humber pilots ruled that any mariner joining the service who had been a master or mate of a steam or sailing vessel of 1,000 tons or upwards, would start as a first class pilot, which gave him a distinct advantage over licensed pilots of lower grades who had come in with the same qualifications earlier.

Dissatisfaction was so great in the Humber district that pilots formed the Humber Pilots' Mutual Protection Society to represent them and put their case to the Commissioners. Discontent about these matters existed all through the Service with the result that the United Kingdom Pilots' Association was formed in 1884 to look after the interests of all pilots at national level, and this Association later became one of the consultative bodies used by the Board of Trade (now the Department of Trade) on any matters relating to pilotage (See Appendix D).

Eventually, in 1888, a Select Committee was set up to consider the position of the Pilotage Service in the United Kingdom. A great deal of evidence was presented to the Committee by pilots and others. Commander Cawley, who had been appointed the first President of the U.K. Pilots' Association, gave important and valuable evidence based on his long experience and knowledge, arguing the case most convincingly.

Some changes in the law were made as a result of the Committee's Report and these were incorporated in the Act of 1890. Masters were no longer given certificates as first class pilots on entering the service, and the law was amended to prevent unlicensed pilots being employed. The Committee's recommendation that pilots should have direct representation on all pilotage boards was put into effect, but masters and mates were still to be granted certificates in certain circumstances, as were aliens.

Discussion on compulsory pilotage continues, though the Department of Trade recommend that, as a general principle, pilotage should be compulsory subject to some carefully considered exemptions (see Appendix A).

H.M. ships have always been free of pilotage but Clyde pilot George Howison says that they find their services are required by the Queen's ships occasionally, especially in foggy weather, and the Ministry of Defence ought to pay their share towards costs of maintenance of pilotage services.

In 1906 the Government prohibited the issue of pilotage certificates to aliens, with the exception of certain long-standing ferry services, but the Pilotage Act places no nationality restrictions on granting pilots' licences although many bye-laws restrict them to British subjects. However, the Department's statement that "these provisions may need to be considered in the light of E.E.C. obligations" has caused some comment. In a letter printed in *The Pilot* of January 1976, Mr A. R. Boddy, a Harwich pilot, points out that while it may be reasonably acceptable to some pilots working in E.E.C. countries, if done on a reciprocal basis, it would be absolutely intolerable to others. He argues that British shipping has never really concerned itself with the short sea trade and that Germans, Dutch and Danes have more North Sea trade vessels entering British ports than there are British ships entering theirs. If pilotage certificates were issued to foreigners in Holland it would be likely that foreign certificate holders would pay the full pilotage charge as Dutch certificate holders do now. In any case, Dutch pilots being civil servants and not self-employed as the British, receive their full salary whether or not they pilot the vessel, so long as it pays. He also draws attention to the fact that most German and Danish pilotage districts have never had compulsory pilotage, hence vessels whose masters would apply for pilotage certificates presumably do not take pilots now and thus no pilot's living is affected. Even the Department's qualification that "all certificate holders should have fluent command of English" would not be worth much since the international language of the sea is English.

While pilots, like other self-employed people, may contend strongly for their right to the job, they are nonetheless ready to serve in an emergency even though it may be outside their terms of employment, as is evidenced by the many accounts of pilots and pilot cutter crews effecting rescues.

An accident to a passenger hovercraft occurred off Southsea in March 1972, when the Southsea-Ryde hovercraft capsized in rough seas in a wind reported at forty-five miles an hour. Trinity House pilot vessel *Vigia* was first on the scene, arriving one minute before the first helicopter. In spite of manoeuvring problems in heavy seas sixteen people were rescued from the upturned hovercraft and taken to Portsmouth, after which the pilot boat returned to the scene and remained until the search was called off that evening. At the end of the same year a hovercraft collided with the British Rail ferry in thick fog, half a mile off Ryde, sustaining substantial damage; the skirt was ripped, the propeller twisted and twelve feet of hull split open. This time the pilot lanuch *Valonia* rescued eight passengers while another pilot boat—the *Valid*— towed the hovercraft back to Ryde.

Another member of the Trinity House Pilotage Service was awarded a medal for rescuing a colleague when he fell from a motor boarding boat off Harwich at the end of

1970. The boat was transferring pilots from the *Penlee* to the *Preceder* when the accident occurred. The seamen leapt into the water and kept the boarding boat and the *Preceder* apart, saving his colleague from being crushed.

Many more incidents could be cited. In a speech delivered in 1906, in the House of Representatives, the Hon. Stephen Sparkman, of Florida, spoke for all pilots when he said:

"No skilled vocation or profession performs so much and obtains so little from the great interests they serve. Facing danger, often beyond the hope of relief, risking life for the cause they serve, they are ever at the post of duty."

Trinity House pilot vessel *Vigia*.   *Brook Marine Limited*

CHAPTER SEVEN

Pilot Craft

PRIOR to the passing of the Act of 1766 establishing the Liverpool Pilot Service, Liverpool pilots were not subject to any authority; they were unlicensed and self-employed, owning their own boats. As soon as a ship hove in sight they began a mad race to sea in an endeavour to be the first to offer to pilot the ship to the port. Sloops and cutters could often be seen seventy miles outside the Bay racing to get the pilot on board a sailing ship before its rivals, each charging whatever rate he could obtain, undercutting one another in order to take the ship. Often they spent long hours at sea watching and waiting for the arrival of ships which, at that time, had no means of advising their expected time of arrival.

In Liverpool in the late eighteenth century, less than half a million tons of shipping was being served annually by about 50 pilots and ten pilot cutters which were less than 40 feet long and of only 30 tons. Three of these small pilot boats were wrecked in 1770 with the loss of 28 lives, the greater number being pilots.

The *Two Brothers* was inward bound to Liverpool on a dark night when a violent east-north-east gale blew up and the boat struck Hoyle Bank. With crew and passengers exposed to the elements, nine of them took to the punt and although it was immediately swamped by the waves, they managed to haul it up on the bank. Eventually they dragged the punt over the bank and launched her in a channel leading to the River Dee, where she drove before the wind until she struck the beach. Five of the occupants had already perished from cold, fright or fatigue. Two pilots and a passenger who survived were too exhausted to crawl out of the punt. The ninth occupant of the ill-fated boat was a pilot who attempted to get help from another pilot boat, but although his urgent distress calls were heard, it was impossible to help.

It may seem strange to read of passengers on board a pilot boat, but at that time it was customary for the boats to take back to port friends of the passengers or crews who were outward bound.

Another pilot boat, carrying five pilots, was missing on the same day and never found.

Towards the end of that disastrous year the most recently acquired boat, *The Prudence,* was wrecked off Conway. The losses on this occasion not only included the master but one of the three survivors of the *Two Brothers* lost a month earlier.

All boat owners received the same share from the money earned for the use of their boat, but some pilots were replacing losses with boats which were too small and sailed badly. After considering several different proposals it was decided that nine boats, each of 40 tons, to carry a master, six or seven pilots and two or three apprentices, would be appropriate and this ruling was added to the byelaws.

When the Mersey Docks and Harbour Board was formed in 1858 there were 12 boats served by 200 pilots, while shipping had increased to 9,000,000 tons. Today's cutters are of 700 tons and carry four times as many pilots, serving more than 30,000,000 tons.

These boats are no longer owned by the pilots but by the Mersey Docks and Harbour Board. With ever increasing costs, most other authorities have either taken over ownership or provided considerable subsidies.

The fleet of the Liverpool Pilotage Service today comprises two diesel-electric-station-keeping pilot boats, and four fast diesel tender launches. Two boarding stations are maintained for the purpose of putting on board or taking pilots off ships. The outer station is based ashore at Point Lynas, Anglesey, where the majority of inward vessels receive their pilots. The inner station is maintained in the vicinity of the Bar Lightship, fifteen miles from Liverpool. This is the threshold of the main buoyed channel leading into the River Mersey.

Each of the two pilot boats takes its turn of seven days duty at the Bar Station and seven days in dock for maintenance. They are manned by a crew of eight or nine apprentices with two pilots as masters, are capable of accommodating 20 pilots and are fitted with all modern aids to navigation. Punts on davits are lowered into the water to take pilots to the incoming ship.

Two fast diesel launches, *Puffin* and *Petrel,* used as tenders for transporting pilots to and from the Bar station, are manned by a crew working in twelve hour shifts and consisting of master, engineer and two able bodied seamen. These launches are capable of carrying 16 pilots. They are powered by Rolls Royce engines with a speed of 16 knots and fitted with radar, R/T's, V.H.F. radio and echo sounder. They are big sea-going launches and can work at gale force nine.

Pilots are boarded and taken off vessels at Point Lynas, 55 miles from the port, by two 21-knot, 40 foot launches manned by a crew of two.

The Corporation of Trinity House London owns a fleet of pilot cutters, fast launches and ancillary craft which operates in the London, Isle of Wight and Falmouth districts. Pilot cruising cutters are being replaced, wherever possible, by fast shore-based launches. It has been found that cutters are expensive to maintain and build, and pilots often spend many wasted hours on board waiting for ships requiring their services.

In 1957 the cutter stationed at the Needles entrance to Southampton was replaced by fast launches based at Totland, Isle of Wight. Other pilotage authorities, in this country and abroad, have followed the example of Trinity House in this matter. Folkestone, Harwich and Margate are using them. The *Lodesman,* a 70-foot cutter with a steel hull, built in Holland, is a good heavy weather boat in service at Folkestone. She was purchased to maintain the reputation pilots have of being able to provide a pilot whatever the weather.

The cruising cutter *Pathfinder*, with a length of 175 feet and gross tonnage 678, is the remaining large pilot vessel used at the Sunk Pilot Station. She cost half a million pounds to build and when she took up her station at Dover on 22nd February 1955 she was described as the latest and finest ship built for Trinity House. She can carry up to 24 pilots and has a crew of 18. Pilots are transferred to ships requiring their services by means of the 18 foot

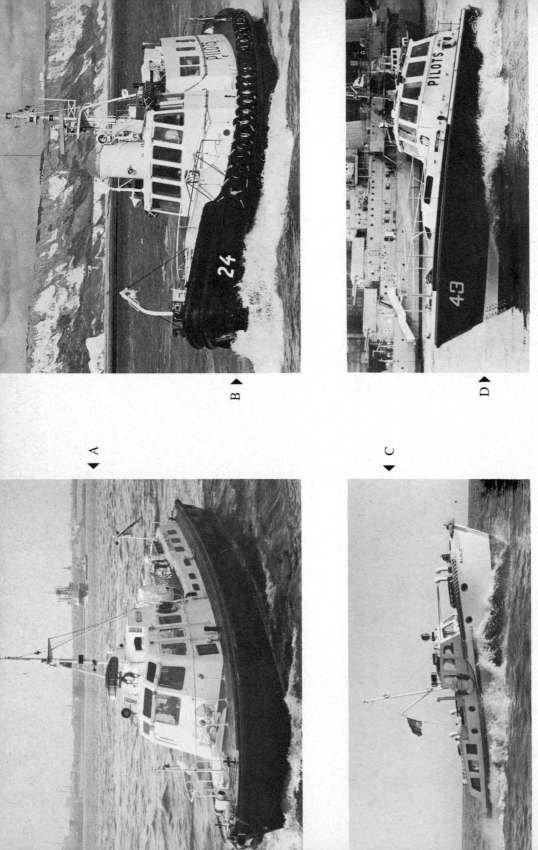

Pilot Boats. A. Liverpool pilot boat *Puffin* (*Mersey Docks & Harbour Board*); B. Launch *Lodesman* at Folkestone Pilot Station (*D. A. McDonald*); C. 35 foot *Bijilo* built for Gambia (*Brook Marine*); D. 50 foot Halmatic launch *St Clement* (*Halmatic*).

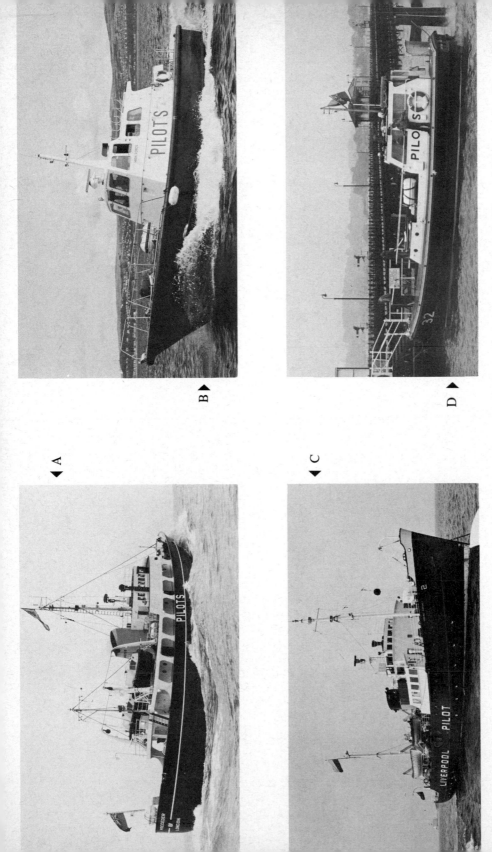

Pilot Boats. A. 139 foot *Preceder* (*Brooke Marine*); B. Tees Pilot cutter *High Force* (*Tees Pilot Cutter Co.*); C. Liverpool Pilot boat No. 2, *Edmund Gardner* (*Mersey Docks and Harbour Board*); D. The 40 foot *Valour* at Ryde pier (*Halmatic*).

motor boats which are normally turned outboard ready for lowering. *Pathfinder* remains at the Sunk for up to twelve weeks at a time.

The tender *Preceder* takes out pilots and relief crews to the Sunk Pilot Station; also oil, water, stores and laundry.

Pilots place tremendous reliance in coxswains of launches, officers of cutters, and boatmen in motor boarding boats, who are specially selected and trained.

Pilot boats are built in consultation with pilots. They must be very good sea boats; speed is increasingly important. In some outports Trinity House underwrites bank loans to keep the boats in action and in some ports the pilot, on joining the service, signs a form stating that he is a shareholder in the boats. Shipping and landing fees vary from port to port and pay for the upkeep of the boats. In small ports the pilots themselves maintain them and ensure that there is always one available to ship a pilot.

Pilots at Exmouth also have a share in the cutter, any new pilot being appointed has to take over the previous pilot's share which is now valued at £425. The shipowner has to pay £7 every time the pilot comes out to bring in a ship, that is £14 for inward and outward journey.

Pilot vessels at The Nab and the Needles pilot stations only put to sea when their services are required so that it is essential that advance notice of the need for the service of a pilot is given. As an indication of the activity of the eight pilot launches in the Isle of Wight district, during 1974 the total fuel taken was 89,916 gallons, while the estimated total mileage run was 144,749, an average run per ship being 21.04 miles.

Most pilot boats are equipped with radio communication for passing operating instructions and information with pilot stations and offices ashore and ships at sea.

Well over thirty different boat builders in all have built the boats used in the United Kingdom pilot service. Brooke Marine Limited is one of the boat builders supplying pilot cutters of high quality. The design of their 50-foot fast pilot cutter is developed from the 44-foot lifeboats built by the R.N.L.I. *Gore Point*, in use at King's Lynn, is a good example of these. The hull is constructed of all-welded mild steel with built-in, double-bottom fuel and oil tanks, sub-divided into five watertight compartments. Sea-water-resistant aluminium alloy has been used for the superstructure. The wheelhouse is totally enclosed with opening windows and all-round visibility, while navigational equipment includes radar, echo sounder, compass, searchlight and foghorn. The engine room, with its twin diesel engines, is also totally enclosed and watertight, with access from the galley.

The Halmatic Company have built over 200 pilot boats for twenty countries, including France, Belgium, Sweden, Holland, Italy, Denmark, Australia, Canada, South Africa, Nigeria and the Middle East. All countries tend to favour the common shape and pattern but specialise in different colours. For example, Danish are blue, Swedish orange and Australian are yellow and orange. In the United Kingdom the law requires that the hull is black.

The *Vigia*, which has now been in service for over ten years with Trinity House was the first pilot boat to use a Halmatic 40-foot hull and has done 300,000 miles. She is a G.R.P. (Glass Reinforced Plastic), twin-screw, semi-displacement boat. Initially she served as a ferry between East Cowes, the Isle of Wight and the pilot cutter stationed off the Nab Tower, but is now based at Ryde pilot station and provides an all-weather, round-the-clock service, shipping and landing pilots for ships in the Solent. In 1969 a fire in the engine room caused extensive damage and was so intense that it cracked her hull. She was taken to the Automarine Yard at Bembridge for repair which, when completed, was virtually imperceptible. The hull suffered no loss of strength and has given satisfactory service ever since.

The Halmatic 50-foot design, now in service with Trinity House, has capacity for eight pilots, is of outstanding seaworthiness, has stout rubber fendering, sound proofing of the wheelhouse, and ease of handling for the coxswain. Her deck furniture includes a motor-driven pump for fire-fighting and life-saving equipment; the guard rails are in position for easy access and the deck layout has been planned for ease of shipping the pilot. The narrow pointed superstructure allows a good angle of roll without causing damage. There is the usual equipment, such as radar, V.H.F., pilot lights and a searchlight.

This boat took three years to develop and was the culmination of eight years of experiments in pilot boats, the emphasis of the design being on safety.

Halmatic 40-foot pilot boats have a capacity for four to six men and normally have two life-rafts which are inflated automatically. The wheelhouse is midships or aft with a radar scanner on top. There are two diesel engines and indicators to inform the coxswain if the watertight door down to the engine room is open. Deck fittings are in phosphor bronze or galvanised iron. These boats have capacity for 300 gallons of fuel oil and 60 to 100 gallons of water.

There have been no accidents to pilots involving fast launches at the Isle of Wight. Safety harness is provided in every boat; a life-jacket being compulsory wear for a seaman when he is on deck. When the pilot comes down the ladder the seaman goes for'd and holds the ladder to make sure that he can help the pilot. He is also instructed to tell the pilot how many steps he has to go. The best time for the pilot to board from the launch is often when it is at the top of the sea.

It now takes five months to build a 50-foot Halmatic launch and four to five months to build the 40-foot type. One of the requirements of Trinity House is that the starboard and port engines should be totally independent of each other so that, in the event of trouble with a battery or fuel tank, it is possible to return to base on the alternative engine. When the engines are linked there is risk that water might get into the fuel tanks and put both engines out of action; with no technicians on board it is considered better to come in on one engine if necessary rather than try to discover how to make the changeover with only two crew on board.

When boarding, Trinity House pilots tend to drive their boat hard against the ship's side. As a result there is considerable impact damage; the fendering is often ripped off and replaced but Trinity House regard this as an expendable item.

Pilot cutters have been damaged or sunk on a number of occasions. The following two instances are examples of the risks run by pilots and boat crews even before the pilot has boarded the ship to bring her safely to port.

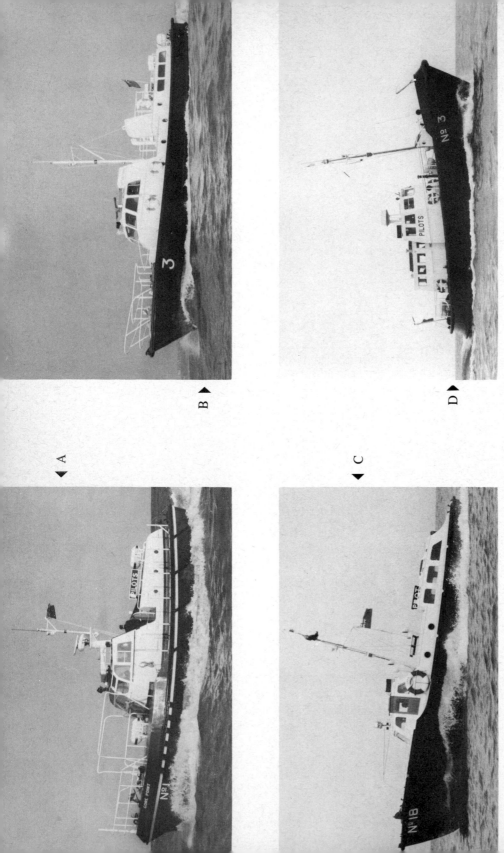

Pilot Boats. A. 50 foot cutter for King's Lynn Conservancy Board; B. 65 foot *Captain Sibree* built for Humber Pilots; C. The 36 foot Trinity House *Vectis*; D. The Preston Pilots' *Saint Joan.*

Brooke Marine Limited

In February, 1956, the Hull pilot launch was in collision with the *Tattershall Castle* as she was leaving Victoria Pier at Hull for New Holland. She had only moved about 150 yards towards the river when danger threatened and the pilot launch and ferry boat gave alarming blasts on their hooters. With astonishing suddenness the *Tattershall Castle* tore a gaping hole through the side of the pilot launch and the mate engineer came out of the engine room to see the ferry boat towering above them. The captain of the pilot boat was in the wheelhouse when he saw the imminence of the *Tattershall Castle.* It was too late to get out of the way; even while he was trying to avoid a collision the bows of the ferry boat crashed into the side of the launch. Water was pouring into the boat as passengers and crew of the ferry boat watched. Quickly the captain and crew of the pilot boat raised a ladder to the forepeak of the ferry and, amid a cloud of steam, pilots and crew climbed up to the deck of the ferry. Almost immediately the pilot launch sank, fortunately with no loss of life.

Nearly seven years later another Humber pilot cutter, the *J. H. Fisher*, thirty-one years old and a floating base for pilots, was holed amidships by a tanker, the *Esso Glasgow.* The accident happened before dawn on a cold January morning in thick fog and a snow squall. Only those on watch or next in turn for pilot duties were awake. Most of the pilots and crew were asleep in their bunks when whistles sounded and the klaxon horn hooted as, with a splintering of wood, the tanker hit the motor boat on the port side. The *Esso Glasgow's* bow went into the engine room of *J. H. Fisher* and water came gushing in. Feverishly the men began to plug the hole with mattresses and blankets. When these proved unsuccessful the captain ordered his 22 crew and 18 pilots to abandon ship. Then he put out a Mayday call. 14 pilots and 15 crew were picked up by the tanker and eventually landed in Hull by a Grimsby tug. The captain and 10 men stayed to make a last minute bid to save the cutter, but to no avail. Two pilot apprentices were among the 11 men who stayed to the last. The men clambered down the ropes into an inflatable life raft and only just had time to get on to the raft before the cutter sank. Visibility was down to about 500 feet as the men left the ship.

An hour after the cutter had sunk one of the last of the pilots to leave her was back on duty. While on his way to Spurn Point in the pilot motor boat, a Russian ship signalled for a pilot to take her up the river. As it was his turn for duty the pilot was transferred to Spurn lifeboat from which he boarded the Russian vessel.

Before the rescue operation was completed the Humber Pilotage Authority was recalling pilots from leave to form an emergency crew to man the other cutter at Spurn Station.

Similar incidents with pilot boats have occurred in other countries. America's early history of the mad race to the sea is similar to that of the United Kingdom, but, as with the British, this was eliminated with the operation of the rotation system and the formation of pilot associations in the different states, which were firmly established in 1882. This resulted in pilots pooling their interests and sailing their boats on a co-operative plan so that, instead of six or eight pilots owning a small boat, the whole body of pilots of a port owned one or two large boats.

When pilotage became compulsory at the Port of Sydney, New South Wales in 1833,

Trinity House pilot vessel *Pathfinder* on station.

each pilot owned his own whaleboat and employed his own crew. Competition was fierce and often pilots were away in their boats for two days on the lookout for a ship. When the ship *Edward Lombe* was wrecked in August 1834, as a result of which 12 lives were lost, a new system was introduced for manning the boats. Pilots then boarded ships at night, weather permitting, from boats which were moored alongside the Sow and Pigs Lightship *Rose,* later replaced by the *Bramble.* When a boat went off to a ship its place was taken by another at the lightship. After still further losses sailing pilot vessels were adopted and a three-masted schooner carrying a master, a mate and 10 seamen took over this duty in 1862. Later a second schooner was built with masters and crews accommodated on shore. These schooners, however, were unsuccessful and were taken off after only two years. In 1953 the diesel electric ship *Wyuna* was designed and built for the pilots. This vessel could remain outside for six months without refuelling.

In his book, *Port Phillip Pilots and Defences*, Captain J. Noble describes a tragedy in August 1927 when two seamen left the anchored pilot steamer *Victoria* to pick up a pilot.

"Tide was ebbing strongly and the night was dark. Unable to make progress against the tide under oars or sails, the two seamen were again trying to get back to the pilot ship when their boat was swept seawards. Their shipmates aboard the *Victoria* were unaware that the boat had not reached the shore safely. In the swirling Rip the boat capsized, lost oars and sails, but the two men hung on until another sea turned it right side up again. Throughout the cold stormy night the two men crouched in the boat with no food or means of propulsion, fighting for survival.

Meanwhile, aboard the *Victoria* it was not known that the boat was missing until the outside steamer, *Akuna*, came in to Queenscliff to investigate the delay. Both steamers and the Queenscliff lifeboat then searched all night without avail.

During the night the elder of the two seamen in the boat died of exposure and the survivor drifted helplessly in the waterlogged boat. After an ordeal lasting thirteen hours the boat was cast ashore near Sorrento, and he collapsed on the beach. He was eventually found wandering in the scrub near Rye."

In South Australia the replacement of certain of the older and slower vessels with new 20 knot vessels of approximately 40-feet in length is under consideration. There is a widespread trend here, as in other countries, to adopt this type of fast vessel for pilot service duty, but to use small and more economical vessels for the transfer of pilots to and from ships.

Port Adelaide was the only port at which a residential pilot stations was maintained, and due to improved communications and fast reliable transport, the use of this station has been discontinued and all pilots now operate from their homes.

No pilot of any country will refuse service when distress calls come within the range of their responsibilities. Pilots, as other seamen, have responded to such calls with a total disregard of self-interest and their own safety and many have given their lives in peacetime as well as in war to rescue life and property at sea.

Trinity House, London Coat of Arms.

TRINITAS IN UNITATE

Corporation of Trinity House,
London.

CHAPTER EIGHT

Tugs — Their Function

THESE are provided for the safety and convenience of ships using the waterway or berthing and unberthing; in many ports their use is essential while in others tug assistance greatly improves speed and safety in manoeuvring. They are especially useful in controlling the ship in strong wind and current conditions.

The increasing size and draught of ships has had its effect on the tug business. Bigger ships require greater bollard pull and the old tugs had either to be replaced or adapted to meet the new requirements. Some tug companies have found it quite satisfactory, as well as cheaper, to adapt.

Tugs play a vital role in bringing ships into port; their manoeuvring power and steering ability when running astern are an important factor in good berthing. Small ships, in the main, do not require them but large ships do, in fact the bigger the ship the greater the need. In Southampton five tugs are normally required for very large tankers, occasionally six, while three or four are used for berthing container ships. When sailing one or two less are used except in high winds or other unusual circumstances.

In tidal docks and confined channels they may be needed at each end of the ship to work her into locks, round narrow bends or through gateways in docks while entering or leaving a berth, to prevent damage by striking the dock side. In such operations the ship is virtually under the control of the tugs, the ship's engines only being required to check or gain headway or sternway or to assist in swinging.

One of the places where tugs are essential for the larger ships is on the confined waters of the Manchester Ship Canal. Navigation of big ships in any artificial waterway is vastly different from that in the open sea, creating its own particular problems by the action or motion of the ship. This does not imply that navigation of the Canal is exceptionally difficult or unsafe, merely that there must be recognition of the effect of space and manoeuvring limitations. Casualties have been infinitesimal.

The pilot and tug master need to be aware of the precautions to be exercised regarding currents and winds; the effects produced on the water by other vessels, especially when passing; or when entering or leaving locks, bridges, rock cuttings and rounding bends or curves. The pilot may decide to use one or more tugs at each end of the ship in such circumstances, for it is normal for the pilot to advise the master of the number required. As in Liverpool, however, the final decision on the number of tugs to be used rests with the ship's master. In Liverpool there were problems with very large ships, but powerful tugs are now used and it is seldom that there is disagreement about the number required.

The efficient handling of tugs is a highly specialised craft; a good tug master hardly needs directions from the pilot. He is always on the alert, keeping the head tug on the

Making fast a tug to the Greek tanker *Mary Livance* prior to berthing at Shell Haven.   *D. A. McDonald*

middle of the Canal, checking and bringing the vessel straight when she tends to sheer. Pilot and tug masters must determine the canal temper of a steamer, that is, the conditions and rate of speed under which she will best navigate the Canal. This must be arrived at after careful observation, and kept in mind during the voyage, rate of speed being a most important factor, varying with different vessels and even with the same vessel under different conditions, the success of the passage largely depending on it. Excessive speed can disturb the water to such an extent as to be a source of danger to the vessel itself as well as to others in the Canal whether they are underway or just moored. Its effect is to drive the water ahead of the vessel so that it rises several inches higher for a few miles in some instances, thereby leaving it that much lower astern and creating such pressure on the ship's bow that it becomes almost impossible to prevent her going ashore on one or other side of the Canal. At the same time the strain on the mooring ropes of vessels lying at jetties, wharves and quays nearby is such that even the stoutest cannot withstand it and when one rope parts the others will do the same. Conversely, pilots and masters have to be prepared to cope with any emergencies which may arise should other ships be moving towards them at high speed.

Tugs are occasionally used in Dover Straits to assist ships to manoeuvre in this busy channel. In open harbours, where there is usually more navigable room than in docks, it is more convenient to work the ship to her berth under her own devices. If tugs are used they are mainly employed to assist the ship into her place during the last stages, or to tow her out from a mooring which would otherwise be difficult to leave. They may be used to push the ship into position, to pull her, or merely hold her in position.

By contract the ship is responsible for any damage to tugs from the time of leaving the wharf to attend the ship until their return. In ship handling the tug is regarded as an extension of the ship she is towing.

Many services are required of tugs. Large, ocean rescue tugs are stationed at various ports to bring ships which have been damaged at sea into port. Many such vessels would have been lost at sea had tugs not gone to their aid.

The tug tender takes passengers out to large liners, while a medium-sized tug may pull heavy loads up the river.

One of the more recent operations to which pilots are assigned is the piloting of oil rigs to their respective oil fields. On 29th June, 1974 *Graythorn I*, the immense B.P. oil rig, was towed out to sea prior to its placement on the sea bed in Fortis Field as Britain's first North Sea Oil production platform.

Control console in the wheelhouse of Offshore Marine's *Shetland Shore* (5000 h.p.), July 1976.

Offshore Marine Limited

Tug assistance for the berthing of the 207,332 ton Shell tanker *Medora* at Shell Haven. Four tugs were employed, each in the range 2000—2500 IHP.   *D. A. McDonald*

Perched on a small wooden platform erected on the front of the rig, and with a plotting table immediately beneath him, Gerald Coates, (Tees pilot and member of U.K.P.A. Executive) piloted the 400-foot long structure, with dimensions of 275 feet by 230 feet, down the mile long Seaton Channel with only about 10 metres clearance on either side when in position on the centre line of the channel.

A similar operation was performed a few months later when *Transworld 58* was taken to Argyll Field. Five Tees pilots, one in each of the large tugs, were engaged in the task, with Graham Blackler on the rig. He was disembarked in the dark in Tees Bay, being lowered about 150 feet by crane.

Tug companies throughout the country hire their craft to shipowners as required. At Gravesend two tug companies combined as London Tugs Limited and purchased the Royal Terrace Pier on which they and the pilots rented their office, and which has served shipping for over one hundred years. Since its purchase it has been adapted and expanded enabling the tug company to secure for themselves a proper deep-water station so that they cease to be the tenants and are now the owners, while the pilots have a big new station.

In Australian ports most of the towage services are supplied by private contractors, but in New Zealand the Harbour Board supplies all plant and equipment needed to operate the pilot service and also employs personnel including pilots.

In Victoria, Port Philip sea pilots own, operate and administer their own company, but pilot rates are controlled by the Marine Board and are relatively the same as in other Australian States.

Harbour craft, of which there are many different varieties, generally come under the surveillance of the Harbour Master in any country. Lighters are used for taking goods from one part of the river or docks to another. Dredgers, of course, are essential in most harbours. These are kept busy removing the silt deposited on river beds. During more recent years they have been much occupied making berths deeper so that they may accommodate larger ships.

Tugs are required in some large ports to move floating cranes into position. These are mounted on big pontoons, and used for lifting heavy cargo or for placing dockside equipment into position. Bunkers carrying oil fuel for ships' engines, small tankers used for carrying fresh water to ships in harbour, fire floats and launches of various kinds for the use of harbour masters, river police and other personnel using the harbour are among the great variety of things and people to be seen in the harbour when pilots bring in the ships with their heavily laden cargoes.

Oil rig *Transworld 58* being taken to Argyll Field with five pilots, one in each of five large tugs and Graham Blackler on the rig. *E. F. Hicks*

CHAPTER NINE

Pilot Stations

PILOTAGE in the United Kingdom is operated by about 40 different pilotage authorities (see Appendix B), each responsible for their own district, though ultimate control and decisions on important issues rests with the Department of Trade, which makes all pilotage orders.

London district has four main stations at Dover/Folkestone, Harwich, Sheerness and Gravesend. There are 680 Trinity House pilots, of whom 450 are in the London district, with five different classes, namely:—

River Thames: Gravesend to London Bridge and vice versa
Channel: Gravesend to the Sunk Cutter or to Folkestone
Inward (South):   Folkestone to Gravesend
Inward (North):   Sunk pilot cutter to Gravesend or
                    Cork light vessel to Harwich and Felixstowe
River Medway: Sheerness to Rochester Bridge and vice versa
                    and to Sunk Cutter and Folkestone

Until recently the pilot station at Gravesend was on the Royal Terrace Pier which had been used by pilots soon after it was opened in 1834, when it became a favourite landing place for royalty. When, in 1892, it had become unsafe and the pilots were given notice to leave, they determined to find the money to purchase and restore the pier. Pilots themselves subscribed the sum of £12,000, significant of the value they attached to retaining it as a pilot station. With additional funds and the assistance of Trinity House, the necessary work was done and the Royal Terrace Pier Estate Company Limited was formed with the condition that shareholders must be pilots; later this included pilots' widows. Plans included the provision of pilots' accommodation and a steel bridge extending 100 feet into the river with a floating stage to attract the steamboat trade.

Work was completed and the new pier was officially opened on 6th June, 1894. In his speech at the opening ceremony Captain Vyvyan, an Elder Brother of Trinity House, said the pilots should be complimented as "had they not proceeded it is doubtful whether Gravesend could have been maintained as a pilot station."

For seventy-two years this prospered until, in the early 1960's, with younger pilots not prepared to buy shares, and the amount of money needed for its restoration and modernisation, it was sold to the joint tug companies (now amalgamated as London Tugs Limited), who had their offices on the pier as tenants.

As a result the Gravesend Pilot Station is now housed in a building opened in 1976 by H.R.H. the Duke of Edinburgh in his capacity of Master of Trinity House. The second and third floors are used by the pilots and radar and V.H.F. are installed. The pilots'

Pilot cutter *Vedette* entering Folkestone.

D. A. McDonald

operations room is cantilevered out over the river to improve the view. Twelve cabins are provided for pilots.

The station is on service for twenty-four hours a day every day, with a duty pilot working a roster system and with River and Channel pilots on watch who are available immediately they are called. The port may be entered at any time but fog warnings are broadcast by the Port of London Authority. Only three generations ago messengers were sent on horseback to pilots' houses to call them for duty; later they were sent on bicycles. They knocked on the door of the house saying: "Pilot, you are on duty." Twenty-five to fifty years ago many pilots did not live more than half a mile away from the station. Now, with modern communications and easy travel by car, they can live further away and still be at the station in ten to fifteen minutes from the time they are called by telephone. Whether or not any ships are expected, there are sufficient men on the station to deal with any emergency. The Channel pilots' roster is made up at ten o'clock each morning from a return book which runs from midnight to midnight.

Many people think that there has been a greater change in shipping in the last ten years than there was in the previous one hundred years. Ten years ago Gravesend pilots could take as many as ninety ships on one night; today's average is about 50 per cent of this figure. One reason for this is the change which has taken place in the size of ships. Cargoes previously loaded by hand are now carried in containers 20 to 40 feet long and the seamen have no idea what is in them. One container ship of 28,000 tons gross will carry a cargo which would have been handled by 21 ships in the past.

Ships of 200,000 deadweight tons, 1,100 feet in length, and 45 feet draught, are regularly berthed at Thames Haven and come into Gravesend Reach to tank clean at Tilbury in light condition. Bulk carriers of 650 feet length, tankers of 750 feet and 36 to 38 feet in draught proceed to Dagenham where the width of the navigable channel is only guaranteed at 600 feet. Some ships carry only motor cars, others nothing but grain or cement which is pumped into the ship and sucked out at the other end. Timber was formerly a seasonal trade. Now it is cut to uniform length and made up into parcels, each parcel fitting into the other as it is lifted on to the ship.

Old time pilots had to contend with under-powered vessels weaving in and out of sailing barges, tugs, tows and lighters. Modern pilots handle ships which, when turning in the tideway, block the river and, were it not for the knowledge which pilots have acquired, both from their training and practical experience, the Thames could be paralysed.

Folkestone is an Inwards South station and part of the London district, piloting ships to Gravesend or Sheerness. There they come ashore and make their way home. They work to an alphabetical roster.

Until 1967 they worked from a cruising cutter but these were expensive to maintain and proved to be uneconomic. Pilots at Dungeness might wait forty-eight hours or more before being called. Also it was difficult to keep the cutter supplied with pilots in bad weather.

For these reasons, and after trials of a fast 40-foot and 20 knots type launch, which proved satisfactory in increasing the speed of operation and reduced total operating costs and pilots' waiting time, it was decided to build a shore station at Folkestone and use the 40-foot fast launches to convey pilots to their ship. These launches have now been copied by many other countries, and there are now 18 in use at different Trinity House stations, with more on order.

The cruising cutter *Pathfinder* is still based at Dover and provides pilots for duty off the Sunk, crews changing over each week. After twelve weeks she is relieved and the *Pathfinder* goes back to Dover for maintenance.

The new Folkestone station, costing around £250,000, was started in June, 1969 and completed in 1971. It stands at the south-western limit of the London Pilotage district and completely replaces the cruising cutter which served as a floating hotel for inward pilots awaiting a ship and outward pilots waiting to be landed. During the excavation of the site an unexploded bomb was brought up in the jaws of a grab and the whole of the Folkestone Harbour area had to be cleared while this was made safe.

Now, instead of a large number of pilots having to remain on the cutter in case ships arrive without giving prior notification of their E.T.A. (expected time of arrival), only three pilots are needed to be on station, others being called from their homes shortly before they are required.

The new station is modern in design with clear views across the Channel. Its operations room at the top of the building, at a height of about 70 feet, with its surveillance radars and V.H.F. communications equipment is the nerve centre of the station. Here the duty pilot and his assistant keep continuous watch on shipping movements and maintain a two-way flow of information with ships in the area. They control the shipping and landing of pilots in the Margate North-East Spit area, as well as at Folkestone, regulating the movements of pilot launches and calling out the pilots next on turn for duty.

Cabins are provided for pilots landing or going on duty in the night, also for officers and crews of the launches. There is a spacious pilots' lounge and messrooms equipped with hot air convector ovens enabling frozen meals to be cooked in a matter of minutes.

In view of its exposed situation the building has been designed with particular consideration of stability and water-tightness. The windows, which do not open, are protected against rain and sea water, with glass three-quarters of an inch thick at the lower levels, those in the operations room having electrically operated washers and wipers with heating elements in the glass to prevent icing up. Air conditioning is installed and an emergency generator automatically takes over in the event of radar and other vital services being affected by mains failure.

Shoreham is very different. It is one of the smaller outports of Trinity House with only seven licensed pilots against Folkestone's 88. Pilots take ships inwards and outwards and there are no choice pilots and no grades. They take anything over 1,500 tons gross other than British ships on the coast, the largest ship using the port being 6,000 tons deadweight. The watch room, situated on the beach, is small and unpretentious. The pilots pay for this themselves and until seven years ago they provided their own boats. Since then Trinity House has underwritten the cost but pilots still put money into them. They have just acquired a new 34-foot G.R.P. vessel by Halmatic for their use. Prior to that they had two 30-foot pilot boats, the latest of which, *Cheverton*, was built at Cowes, Isles of Wight, seven years ago at a cost of £7,500. The forty-year-old launch, *Osborne,* has been kept in reserve. There is no harbour surveillance, no radar, the cutter sits at the entrance in the lee of the breakwater where ships can be seen.

Shoreham has a difficult tide with a narrow channel and shallow entrance and in bad weather boarding a vessel can be very dangerous. One pilot was lost seven years ago when he went out to board the *Nord Cap,* a German ship with only half a cargo. He went out about nine o'clock at night. A force eight, south-west wind was blowing, causing a big sea. The ship was pitching as the launch came alongside. As the pilot was boarding, ship and launch started to roll towards each other and the pilot was crushed by the cab against the hull of the ship. He lost his grip and fell into the water. Another pilot grabbed him by the coat and managed to hold him, but he had to let go or he too would have been crushed between the launch and the ship. When the launch drifted clear of the ship he grabbed the coat again but it slipped through his fingers and the pilot was gone. His body was recovered three weeks later by a yachtsman fifteen miles along the coast.

Sixty-five per cent of the work at this port is done during the night. A pilot may go out anything from half a mile to five miles to board, depending on the ship.

Southampton is part of the Isle of Wight district, which is an outport of Trinity House. For years the Inward Service was operated by pilots located on the Isle of Wight, while the Outward Service was undertaken by Southampton, but the Inward and Outward pilots have now amalgamated in one service with those pilots who are on duty at any time working both outwards and inwards.

The pilotage service in the district is controlled by a duty pilot from the pilot station at 37 Berth, Southampton. He is responsible for ensuring the proper operation of the service

Trinity House Pilot Station at Folkestone.
D. A. McDonald

to the sub-commissioners of pilotage, a committee representative of local interests who meet once a week and co-ordinate the district under the auspices of Trinity House. He is assisted by a pilotage assistant who collects all orders for pilots from the local shipping agents. They have complete communications coverage of the district which enables them to communicate by V.H.F. radio with the pilot launches operating the Nab and Needles entrances to the Solent and by G.P.O. telephone with the pilots waiting at Ryde Pier, Portsmouth and Yarmouth pilot stations to be transported in the launches. They can also communicate direct with ships either approaching the district and wanting to pick up a pilot or leaving the district and wanting to land a pilot.

There are 64 Trinity House licensed pilots in the district. Two of these are Cowes Harbour pilots and are licensed only to pilot the ships which require pilotage service into and out of Cowes Harbour from Cowes Roads. Another three are Portsmouth Harbour pilots who are licensed only to pilot ships into and out of Portsmouth Harbour from and to the Nab entrance of the district. The other 59 are Southampton and Isle of Wight pilots who are licensed for the whole district and mostly pilot ships between the Nab and Needles and Southampton. However, they also pilot ships into and out of Portsmouth Harbour when the Portsmouth Harbour pilots are unable to cope with the level of work there or are shorthanded due to leave or sickness.

The Southampton and Isle of Wight pilots work on a roster system which involves them in 24 hours on duty and 48 hours off duty when they are in the working roster. Their 24 hours on duty normally entails the pilotage of ships to and from the limits of the pilotage district although they are also occasionally required to cover the duty pilot function and the station pilot function at Southampton to serve those ships which require pilotage services in Southampton Water only.

Pilotage is compulsory with the exception of vessels specially exempted, namely coasters and home traders up to 3,500 G.R.T. Ships enter and leave the district through the Nab and Needles Channels, the Nab being the busiest because it can take the larger ships at most states of the tide. By consulting the British Docks Board sailing lists and Lloyds Lists, and collecting information from shipping agents, pilots know which ships may be expected each day and the approximate time of arrival, but this is only a guide and cannot always be depended on. A ship may develop engine trouble, or be delayed by weather conditions, and arrive a day late. They, therefore, have the facility to communicate direct with the ship by V.H.F. radio when it is two or three hours away from the district. If incorrect E.T.A.s are given this could mean a lot of waiting around with as many as five pilots to land at one time. If a ship calls up and has not previously given an E.T.A. a pilot can usually get to her in three-quarters of an hour. Such delays as do occur in serving a ship are due to ships arriving ahead of E.T.A. or without giving any warning at all. Even such a ship can usually be served within an hour, but pilots encourage ships to give earlier advice of their expected time of arrival which enable pilotage duties to be planned more satisfactorily.

Ships requiring a pilot at the Nab or Needles stations should signal through a Post Office Station to the Ryde Pilot Station twelve hours in advance, if possible, giving their E.T.A. draught and port of destination, stating whether the pilot is required at the Nab or

Needles. A further estimated time of arrival should be sent direct by V.H.F. not later than two hours before arrival and radio contact maintained if it is necessary to vary the E.T.A.

Ships can be brought in to the Solent at most states of the tide, but in bad weather around the Nab station they are asked to come in themselves to more sheltered water so that the pilot can board safely. There are therefore, very few days in the year when vessels are delayed. Deep draughted tankers are usually boarded two or three miles south of the Nab Tower.

Fast pilot launches having good communications and portable radio telephones are available at all three stations. These may be taken on board a ship at the request of the master for operational use by the pilot. Each launch has a 20 w set with a set at each end of the island of about 100 w, and if large ships of over 12,000 tons are diverted, a radio telegram is sent or, if the diversion is to be of three or four hours, the ship is called up on V.H.F. backed up with a radio telegram.

Fifteen crews of two—an officer and a seaman—man the launches. Sleeping accommodation is provided at the Ryde and Yarmouth pilot stations for the benefit of pilots who serve ships during the night and there are facilities for light meals.

The controlling pilot station for the district is at 37 Berth, Southampton. It is situated in the new British Transport Docks Board port operational building, a six storey structure sited at the seaward extremity of the Eastern Docks. It provides centralised operations and communication control for the safe and orderly movement of ships in the approaches to Southampton Docks, with radar coverage of the docks, Southampton Water, Cowes Road and a large area of Spithead and West Solent. The pilot station has workshops for pilot launches, accommodation for pilots and launch crews, administrative offices and a communications and operations room manned by the duty pilot.

Operations room of Folkestone Pilot Station showing the Duty Pilot—at one of the two Decca type R.M.729 radars—and his assistant.   *D. A. McDonald*

Workshops and stores are located on the ground floor, while on the first floor there is a spacious lounge, a well-equipped galley, launch crew cabins, messroom and bathrooms. The pilots' main administration office and the Board Room for sub-Commissioners are located on the second floor; also five well-equipped pilots' cabins, shower and bathrooms. Radar is under the control of the Dock and Harbour Master's department which is situated on the third and fourth floors. A darkened semi-circular operations room on the fifth floor accommodates consoles for six radar displays, chart tables and communications facilities for ships, police and fire services, and has accommodation for the duty pilot and chief operations officer.

The pilot station and Docks Board communications centre are continuously manned. With radar assistance pilots can board ships in the thickest fog. Computers are used with radar to ascertain the positions of vessels, the course and distance the vessel is making, and the nearest approach to a buoy or another ship. This is stored in the memory of the computer so that when an officer comes on watch and wishes to check the position of vessels anchored in Cowes Roads, East or West Solent, he can press the check reference button on the computer and two dots will show against that particular vessel's position.

Those employed in the radar station are not pilots but master mariners with a local knowledge of the area. They hold a radar observer's certificate and are thoroughly conversant with the working of the port, including the berthing of vessels. Four operations officers are employed and two ex-naval signalmen are on watch with them as well as an assistant operations officer when circumstances permit. They operate on a twelve hour watch-keeping system so that the station is always manned and, in poor visibility, pilots can constantly request information from the radar station.

Apart from passing such information to vessels navigating in reduced visibility or in difficult circumstances, the purpose of the station is to co-ordinate the movements of shipping in and out of the port, and to collect and distribute information to all port users. These include immigration, customs, agents and owners, in addition to pilotage and shipping personnel.

With the type of ships and their ever increasing size requiring such precise handling it is essential that pilots and other navigational personnel should be fully acquainted with everything that is taking place within the harbour, the movements of other vessels, restrictions on channel depths and widths and the co-ordination of the flow of movements in and out of the harbour.

There are nearly thirty movements of roll-on/roll-off ships during the summer, falling off by about fifty per cent in the winter. Many 960-foot container ships use the port and there is a weekly average of 800 passenger ship movements in and out of the port during the winter months, increasing to around 1,150 movements per week in the summer. This includes cross-channel ferry traffic, holiday tourist trade, North Atlantic tourist trade and cruising traffic, Southampton being the principal passenger port of the United Kingdom.

The largest type of vessel using the port is the V.L.C.C. which may be up to 300,000 tons deadweight.

The Liverpool Pilot office was moved around a good deal in the late eighteenth century

Outward-bound ships *City of Hull* and *Fremantle Star* converge on THPV *Bembridge* in order to drop their Channel Pilots at the limit of the Pilotage District.　　　　　*D. A. McDonald*

until, in 1795, it was situated in a gaol in Water Street, where it remained for over twenty years. Both the neighbourhood and the place were most unsuitable. Criminals were kept in seven dungeons, six feet square, ten feet underground and the whole place was unsavoury and dirty. Women debtors were kept in a room over the pilot office. Apparently it was necessary to draw attention to the fact that the pilot office was to be found in this place for, in September 1807, an order was given that a large board should be exhibited in front of the building with a pilot boat painted on it and underneath the words "Pilot Office."

After two further moves, the pilot office took over the premises it occupies today, on the Canning Pierhead, North, which bears the date 1883.

The Mersey Docks and Harbour Company is the Pilotage Authority and administers the service through the Pilotage Committee, which is composed of the Vice Chairman of the Docks and Harbour Board, three ship owning members or their representatives, two nautical advisers (retired masters) and three pilots' representatives. The Superintendent of Pilotage is responsible for the day to day operations and office administration. He is on the Pilotage Committee as an executive officer.

A shore-master allocates pilots to ships and sees that a pilot is awaiting a ship on arrival at the Western Station (Port Lynas) or the Bar station. If a ship is leaving the port, or moving in the port, the pilot will go to the place where she lies.

Pilots work on a rota system taking it in turn to pilot ships either inwards or outwards. The majority of the 171 pilots at Liverpool are first class and 46 of these are paid a retainer by various shipping companies. In Liverpool they are known as appropriated pilots. At most other ports they would be described as choice pilots.

Liverpool pioneered a radar station nearly thirty years ago and when the £50,000,000 Royal Seaforth Dock was built a new radar station, 84 feet in height, was erected in the north-west corner. The new station, its seven storeys topped by a striking octagonal observation tower and operations room, 46 feet wide, has an uninterrupted view seawards to the Mersey Bar and upriver to Eastham, and gives a round-the-clock navigational service. There are seven display units and a special computer in the radar room which can store the position of more than 20 ships or objects appearing on the screen at one time.

There is close co-operation between the pilotage service and the Mersey Docks and Harbour Board, especially on administration. The pilotage office is self-contained apart from the accounts, for which pilotage staff use the Docks Board's accounts department and their computer. They also use the same solicitor.

Apart from the pilots and eighty crewmen, a maintenance carpenter for wooden boats and a maintenance engineer are employed. The office staff includes three clerks, a typist, a card girl who processes the pilot cards for the computer, and a telephonist who deal with about two hundred calls a day to send pilots off and bring them in.

As an instance of the shipping activity in the port, pilotage services were about 20,000 in one year while pilotage dues for the same period were over £600,000 with boat rate dues around £430,000. These last are used to pay the Superintendent's salary, keep the crews at sea, pay half the victualling costs, wages, taxes, rail transport, upkeep of the pilot boats and servicing of capital.

Since larger vessels have been using the port, some restrictions are imposed on night navigation. This is prohibited for the 200,000 ton tankers, which are over 100,000 feet long and have a draught of forty-five feet. Regulations provide that, for these, the most difficult part of the channel be navigated during daylight. This poses problems during the winter and restricts movements to eight hours in certain areas, though berthing and leaving the port can be conducted during the night.

The shore pilot station consists of a look-out station manned twenty-four hours a day, a hostel to sleep ten pilots, with lounge, dining room, kitchen and two cottages in the Lynas Lighthouse complex which contains officers' and crew accommodation.

The officer in charge of the Clyde Pilotage Authority, a separate body from the Port Authority, has a staff of 18 who operate and maintain the launches and man the look-out station.

Clydeport, which comprises the port facilities of Glasgow, Greenock and Ardrossan, is owned and administered by the Clyde Port Authority whose headquarters are in Glasgow. A Pilot Master is responsible for pilotage in the district which is compulsory for vessels over 100 tons.

The Clyde can take the largest, fully laden ships in the United Kingdom and Europe. It could possibly handle ships larger than could ever be built. No dredging is required for entry of any of the largest ships from Europe. The net tonnage a year is about 25,000,000 and pilots are expected to do 134 turns per year. When a ship comes in she may go to a discharge berth, then proceed to dry dock for repairs. After repairs she goes to a loading outward berth and from there proceeds to sea. Every time she moves she must have an in and out pilot.

Pilots board incoming vessels at Gourock.

Vessels bound to the Humber requiring the services of Humber Pilots must give advance notice by radio telephone or through a G.P.O. Coast Station to the Spurn Pilot Station, giving estimated time of arrival, draught and destination at least twelve hours in advance. Any adjustment to the time should be given at least two hours before arrival. This

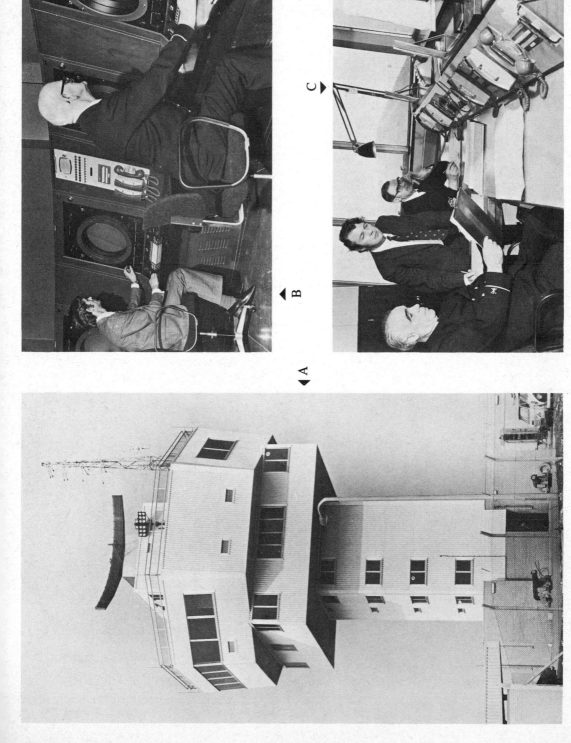

Port of Liverpool's new radar station, at the Royal Seaforth Dock, has a range of 20 miles and is computer assisted. The Port was the first in the world (1948) to provide a radar service for its customers. A. The new station; B. The Radar Room has seven display units (On left is Cris Blake. Assistant Superintendent and George McIntosh, Communications Officer); C. The communications console (Left to right are George Kendall, Senior Communications Officer, Captain Ken Eastwood, Station Superintendent, and Joe Tafe, Communications Officer).

Mersey Docks and Harbour Board

station, with look-out facilities on Spurn Point, was established when the Humber pilot cutter was withdrawn from her cruising station near the Spurn Lightship. Pilot launches operate from this station which is manned by pilots all round the clock.

A Humber bye-law, confirmed by the Department of Trade, requires owners of ships whose masters or chief officers hold pilotage certificates to contribute one-third of the pilotage dues which would have been payable had the master of the ship employed a pilot. Other pilots are agitating for this to be the accepted practice everywhere.

Harwich is in the London Pilotage district. The 126 pilots based there perform 16,000 acts of pilotage a year, while the cruising cutter handles about 11,000 to 12,000 ships a year, sometimes as many as 12 ships coming in for pilotage at a time. This is one of the few districts in the world where pilots have experience of handling all kinds of ships, from really big tankers to motor coasters. A cruising cutter is still in use because of the distance from the cruising station to the base. The Superintendent of Pilots works from an office in the new pilot station at Harwich, and the pilot look-out is housed in the Harbour Conservancy Board's operations room. Here duty pilots work in eight hour shifts, the duty pilot being responsible for giving information to ships and agents about the timing for outward bound ships. The duty pilot also keeps vessels in the harbour advised as to what is happening, such as if a large container ship will be blocking the fairway, advising yachts about visibility and other matters of interest to them. There is also a V.H.F. and radio link with the coastguard.

The duty pilot has an assistant working with him on an eight hour shift, with a slightly different timing so that there is a link with the next pilot coming on duty. These assistants are not pilots; they have naval experience but do not require a master's certificate. Eighteen pilots work on this harbour for a month and then spend five months on the Sunk. They are occasionally sent to Rotterdam or Germany to bring ships into Tilbury.

Whether a few pilots work from a small watch house which they maintain themselves, or many operate from large modern buildings equipped with the latest navigational aids and communications, all are well trained, highly efficient men, devoted to the task of bringing ships speedily and safely to and from their harbours.

The *Liverpool Pilot* and Shell tanker ss *Sepia* with pilot launch approaching tanker.

A Shell Photograph

CHAPTER TEN

Boarding Ships

"CRITICAL errors by skilled people, operating complex machinery, are comparatively rare, accidents are often averted by reason of dedication, skill and effort," wrote Pat Shipley, Lecturer in Engineering Psychology at Birkbeck College, in an article in *The Pilot*, dated August, 1973.

Continually boarding and handling large ships in all weathers needs all these qualities and any pilot who did not possess them could be a very unhappy man, unsuited for the job. No matter what the time of day or night, what his domestic or financial problems may be, how hard winds may blow or storms rage, a turn pilot is expected to be fully awake, alert and healthy, capable of carrying out the physical and mental parts of his work. At a moment's notice, in the middle of a social function, a pilot may be called to go out to a ship. Yet accidents from negligence or inefficiency are rare. All over the world pilotage services are manned by the pick of seafaring men who have been disciplined and trained and are prepared to accept the responsibility of boarding and handling any vessel under almost any conditions.

In a manifesto issued by the United Kingdom Pilots' Association some years ago about the services which a pilot renders, it was pointed out that "by his aid vessels, with their costly cargoes and innumerable precious lives, are brought in safety through black nights and through intricate shoals to the ports they seek." The statement continued—"To the forecastle seamen, rendered anxious, and even fearful, by thick weather and stormy winds, the heaving in sight of the pilot boat is a spectacle almost as welcome as the first glimpse of the shores of his native country. To the shipmaster and to his officers, the coming of the pilot brings a sense of security, a feeling that the vessel is in hands which will surely carry her in safety to her destination."

What then, is required of a pilot and what is his procedure when he is called to board a ship?

A calm confidence in his ability to deal with any situation which might arise does much towards a satisfactory and safe pilotage. This inspires trust in those who have brought the vessel to the boarding station. His sound practical training and long experience of the sea, and particularly of the port, has made the pilot aware of the channels, depths, berths, anchorages, tides, rocks and shoals, as also of other craft using the harbour. He knows and will rigidly adhere to the Rule of the Road, and will be watchful of any who neglect this precaution.

The cruising cutter, when on station with pilots waiting to be called, flies the pilot flag, which is horizontally divided, the top half being white and the bottom half red. Fast launches which take the pilot direct to the ship also display this.

An Outward-bound pilot climbing down into the pilot launch from a Blue Star Liner at the sea-ward limit of the pilotage district.

D. A. McDonald

The master of the vessel requiring the pilot has to bear in mind certain things when approaching the boarding station. He will have notified the pilot station of his E.T.A. and he must know the characteristics and distinguishing marks of the pilot vessel, also the limits of her cruising station, and navigate accordingly, giving the appropriate signals for a pilot in good time. In thick weather he must sound the correct signal and recognise that of the pilot craft.

Whether the ship is being boarded direct from the fast launch or by punt from the cruising cutter, the turn pilot at the top of the roster will be prepared to leave as soon as the signal is given. The launch's coxswain and seaman will be ready for him.

Radio telephone messages may be received by the coxswain while on the way out to board the pilot. It may be a request to try and sight a small ship which the station is unable to contact, or a call on their return trip to pick up other pilots who have taken ships on their outward journey. Occasionally this may mean a slight detour and a wait of fifteen minutes or so. In some ports, such as Harwich, pilots are leaving from and returning to the cruising cutter continuously during the busy season.

Boarding vessels, especially container ships and V.L.C.C.'s presents its own hazards. Inefficient and dangerous ladders, or those insecurely placed, have been the cause of a number of accidents to pilots, even causing death in some cases, although it is remarkable how few there are in comparison with the many movements of ships. Many ports have regulations that cutter seamen must always wear a life jacket when the pilot is about to board, which takes place while the vessel and the pilot boat are moving slightly. Most pilots wear life jackets. The coxswain watches the pilot spring from the cutter on to the ladder—a rope ladder with wooden treads—which may be hanging up to thirty feet down the ship's side. There is a right time to jump depending on the swell. Having seen the pilot board the vessel the seaman attaches the pilot's gear to a rope which has been lowered from the vessel, and this is hauled on board by the ship's crew.

At least one of the crew, and possibly a ship's officer, are waiting to receive the pilot as he climbs on to the deck. It has become a pastime among crew and passengers on liners to make bets about which foot the pilot will use first to step on board.

Ladders on some ships are not always as satisfactory in operation as pilots could wish and crews are often not as careful about the way they put them over the side of the ship. A pilot was leaving a Greek Liberty ship when he noticed the ladder was dragging. He refused to use it and it was taken away but the same ladder was put over again. Halfway down the pilot slipped. Still clinging to the ladder, his arms fully extended, he managed to reach one of the rungs and board the cutter safely, but some have not been so fortunate.

Ten years ago a pilot was drowned at Dover when he fell from an insecure ladder, while another pilot who had joined his ship at Rotterdam fell from a ladder between the ship and the quay. He was knocked unconscious and later died.

It has been estimated that, on average, a pilot is lost in this way each year.

Another tragic incident revealing the risks run by pilots in their devotion to duty occurred on 2nd September, 1974, and was referred to on an earlier page. It will be remembered because the episode was well covered by the media at the time.

Storm force winds swept the West Country and the car ferry *Eagle*, with 170 passengers on board was hit by a heavy wave while at sea. The master decided to abandon the journey to Lisbon, and signalled for a pilot.

A Trinity House pilot cutter went out from Falmouth in response to the ship's signal and the pilot, Captain Laurence Mitchell, was attempting to board her when he fell from the ladder into the sea. Mr Michael Tuffrey, one of the crew of the tug *St Agnes*, dived into the water when the pilot was sighted floating in steep seas. Tugs and a helicopter from Culdrose Naval Air Station joined in the rescue attempt. The helicopter's diver went to the aid of both men but when the pilot was taken ashore by helicopter a few minutes later he was dead.

The pilot of the helicopter commented on the bravery of Mr Tuffrey in attempting the rescue when it was blowing 30 to 40 knots with a spray and white horses and troughs so deep that his diver could not see the tug which was only a few yards away.

The following tribute, written by the pilot's widow, was printed in *The Pilot* in October, 1974:

"My husband was born in Dundee on February 17th, 1925. He was the ninth sea captain in three generations on his mother's side of the family. In Shetland, where he lived for some years, it is traditional for the men to go to sea. . . .

In 1941, before his sixteenth birthday, he was at sea serving his time with Donaldsons on the North Atlantic run. Whisky one way, ammunition the other—could one say "loaded" both ways? He was torpedoed and took to the boats only once in his war career. For a while he served on Canadian ships before gaining his Master's Certificate in 1949. He joined Stephenson Clarke's 'silverbanders' in 1950 so that he could spend more time at home and he was licensed as a pilot on 29th July, 1954 at Portsmouth where all shiphandling, with very rare exceptions, was without tugs. He transferred to Falmouth in 1961 where the big tonnage is, and work is invariably with tugs, so his experience was long and extremely varied. Perhaps the ship he enjoyed piloting most of all was the square rigged training ship *Danmark* when he took her out under full sail for the start of the Tall Ship Race 1966.

Concern for the long term betterment of pilots also absorbed his time and he read and argued long and hard on it. Last year he was given an award for bravery for the rescue of a man and attempting to save the life of a boy. This is how we will always remember him. His life was very rich and all his family is very proud of him."

The editor's comment was: "No more fitting tribute to an active pilot in his prime can be written than by his wife, to whom we offer our profound sympathy and great respect."

Speaking about this incident at the 88th Annual Conference of the U.K. Pilots' Association a year later, the President, the Rt Hon James Callaghan, M.P. said:

"There is no doubt Captain Mitchell knew full well the risk he was taking and the

A pilot cutter makes a close approach to a tanker in order to obtain the maximum possible lee for shipping the pilot.
D. A. McDonald

The 45 foot pilot boat *Kernow* supplied to Falmouth pilots. Maximum speed 12½ knots.

Brooke Marine Limited

difficulties he was incurring trying to board the *Eagle* when she was in distress and needed considerable help. He did that in the very highest traditions of the pilotage service. But it also revealed a need to review carefully boarding arrangements for pilots. The present examination into boarding arrangements must be 'most intense' to ensure that members do not suffer undue risks in carrying out their tasks."

There have also been a number of accidents on pilot hoists, which came into use with the advent of larger ships, no pilot being allowed to climb a rope ladder more than thirty feet high. One of the dangers is the transference from the ladder to the hoist but a far greater problem is their insecurity and failure to function properly due to defects in the equipment and lack of adequate maintenance.

One pilot reports that he was half way up a V.L.C.C. when the hoist stuck and could not be moved up or down. His arms grew weak, it was dark, the pilot cutter had gone and there was no means of communication. With a limited time in which such a position could be maintained, and the strain on the arms becoming greater, the pilot experienced a feeling of panic, especially when he realised that the seaman in charge of the hoist did not know how it worked.

In this case there was no casualty, only a lot of needless mental and physical strain on the pilot.

Rotterdam pilots refuse to use hoists and some ships do not have them. The Norwegians banned hoists on their ships following a near accident when the hoist ran up over the rails in the stopped condition, while the West Germans have banned them until safety devices are fitted.

In Rotterdam, for the past five years, helicopters have been used to drop the pilot on to vessels. Modern ships such as tankers, bulk carriers, and container ships provide for practically ideal air service. Pilot cutters are expensive in manning and repairing but more important is the fact that helicopters save delay. Twenty minutes flying time is equal to four to six hours in a pilot cutter. This method also avoids the risks of boarding by ladders and hoists. Eight hundred vessels a year are serviced by helicopters and they are likely to be used even more in the future.

European pilots have been active in drawing the attention of shipowners and other pilots to required improvements in ladders and hoists. They suggest minimum standards for shipowners to conform to when supplying them to ships. The following letter, with accompanying sketch and form, was published in E.M.P.A. Journal 1974. It was sent to the various European Ministries concerned and also to the Press:

"Sirs, Last year, the pilots of the European Maritime Pilots' Association organised a safety campaign of one week duration to attract the attention of the public and of the authorities concerned on those too numerous ships which jeopardise the safety of shipping and the safety of life at sea because of the deficiency of their crews or of their equipment.

Pilot and Service Engineer joining BP Tanker Company's 215,000 ton *British Explorer* by helicopter off Rotterdam.   *British Petroleum Company Limited*

That safety campaign proved to be a success as the shipowners, who had been duly informed that their ships were likely not to get the services of any European pilot if they did not comply with the Regulations, made a real effort to improve the condition of their vessels. Many deficiencies, however, were reported by the pilots and some ships were delayed until those deficiencies were done away with.

I beg to inform you that the European pilots have decided to engage in another safety campaign which will take place from the 2nd to the 9th February 1974. The pilots will continue to concern themselves with the adequacy of the means of embarking and disembarking which directly affects their own safety, but they will be asked to put greater emphasis on all the deficiencies which might endanger the safety of life or property at large, or constitute a threat to the environment. The defective ships will be reported to the shipowners as well as to the authorities and bodies concerned.

The President, E. Ragazzi
The Secretary, M. Guicharrousse"

"European Maritime Pilots' Association
1 Rue Henri Tasso
13235 Marseille—Cedex 1
France.

Sir,

On the two occasions referred to below, a complaint has been lodged in respect of the

....

....

belonging to your shipping company.

Date	Pilotage District	Nature of Complaint

I am to inform you that unless the subject of these complaints is not put right this ship may not be provided with the services of a pilot in Belgium, France, Germany, Italy, the Netherlands, Portugal, Spain, Sweden and the United Kingdom in which countries the pilots are members of this Association.

Secretary."

United Kingdom pilots, through their Association, have been agitating for a long time for greater safety precautions with ladders and hoists, but until recently little seems to have been achieved internationally.

I.M.C.O. Maritime Safety Committee, at its 27th Session in 1973, approved Recommendations on Performance Standards for Mechanical Pilot Hoists and requested that they be submitted to the I.M.C.O. Assembly for adoption.

A Safety of Life at Sea Conference was held by I.M.C.O. during the last two weeks in October, 1974, the object of which was to improve generally the safety of life at sea in its many aspects. One part of this dealt with the Recommendations made in 1973 concerning pilot hoists (see previous paragraph) and being more stringent than previous regulations, will improve arrangements for pilots boarding or landing from ships if and when the Recommendations are implemented. The Convention was signed on 1st November, 1974 and now has to be ratified by the necessary number of participating governments owning the required percentage of the gross tonnage of world shipping to ensure implementation. It will probably be a further two years before the new pilot ladder regulations become effective. No satisfactory requirements were laid down for pilot hoists but certain general guidelines were accepted.

The three big disadvantages of pilot hoists as used at present, and against which pilots have shown unfavourable reaction are:

(a) When the ladder hangs far below the main deck the spreader on the ladder is of little use, as when the ship lists, the ladder, with the pilot, swings out from the ship's side where it may be caught by the side wind and turned around so that the pilot hangs with his back towards the ship's side. This results in the hoist wires becoming crossed and the pilot hoist as such is therefore partly disabled.

(b) Unfortunate, but necessary, is the requirement that the winch for the pilot hoist must have more than enough wire to lower the ladder when the ship is at her light water line. As it is very difficult for the man manoeuvring the pilot hoist on deck to judge the position of the ladder, it has happened that the ladder with the pilot standing on it, has been lowered into the water and this had resulted in serious injuries to pilots.

(c) Finally, should there be a power failure, the pilot can be left hanging, say 10-15 m below the level of the main deck, without any possibility of helping himself. He simply has to stand on the ladder and wait for help. Many pilot hoists do not have any manual type of operation and this again leaves the pilot in a very exposed, not to say dangerous position.

An article in *The Pilot* of July 1976 draws attention to these three disadvantages before giving the following details of a new system which could materially improve the safety of pilots when boarding ships. The article points out that many manufactureres have been aware of the problems and have tried to make improvements in the design. A Swedish Company (Welin Davit), who have supplied hundreds of ships with pilot hoists, have been working on a new system for use on tankers in the first instance. This is a pilot platform system in which, attached to the lower end of the accommodation ladder is a "pilot platform" fitted with a trap-door and a conventional pilot ladder with a maximum length of

ms *Bohemund* Roll-on/Roll-off Ferry about to embark pilot off Felixstowe.   *Fred Olsen Lines*

9 m. The advantage of this is that the ladder with the always horizontal pilot platform is lowered to the operational position before the pilot boat arrives and the ship's officer in charge has satisfied himself that the equipment is ready for use. The whole thing remains stationary along the ship's side until the pilot is on board the ship. This is now being fitted to many large ships following consultation with their respective pilot organisations and with the approval of the authorities of many of the nations building these large ships.

Reaction from pilots is very favourable as it is the type of equipment which has the safety factor which is so important to them. Another advantage is that the manufacturers have designed the system in such a way as to ensure that the platforms, when in the operational position, will be kept against the ship's side even when the ship is listing. The effect of this is that the conventional ladder on which the pilot climbs from the pilot boat is never far from the ship's side.

Representatives of Trinity House, U.K. Pilots' Association and the Department of Trade inspected this installation aboard a large bulk carrier and found that it measured up to their requirements and expectations.

Although tanker building has ceased at the present time, it is hoped, when certain adjustments are made, that it can be used with container ships, gas tankers and bulk carriers. In these particular ships ladders are almost invariably fitted aft, where the ship curves away, and lead forward so that, when lowered, they reach the quay-side. This position meets with the full approval of the crews, stevedores and others who have occasion to visit the ship because it eliminates the risk of injury due to falling cargo from overhead carriers between the hatch and the quay, but pilots' requirements are that the ladder should lead aft and run for its whole length and at all angles against a vertical ship's side. Not only would the pilot have no support against the ship's side with the ladder positioned aft, but the pilot boat would not be able to lay against the ship's side when both are moving slowly forward and the pilot is embarking or disembarking. It would also be dangerously near the ship's propellers.

An alternative system must, therefore, be devised before the Welin Pilot Platform can be used by pilots to board vessels with a freeboard of more than 9 m.

Various adaptations were considered and it was finally decided to:

(a) replace the ladder by a light frame-work construction
(b) connect the whole system into one unit—davit arms through torque tube to frame-work and platform, the construction being so designed that the centre of gravity of the whole unit is far outboard from the torque tube shafting system when in outboard position. The platform is accordingly pressed against the ship's side when upright and will stay in this position even if the ship lists to about 8-10°, which would be sufficient since pilots would probably not consider embarking or disembarking should the ship heel more than 10°.
(c) The pilot platform itself is in principle of the same type as the previous one, though of a lighter construction and can be fitted with either the 5 m or the 9 m conventional pilot ladder. The main difference is that, after the pilot has climbed up to the platform from his conventional pilot ladder, he no longer walks up the accommodation ladder but stays on the platform together with the ship's officer and is raised to deck level. When disembarking, the platform is again lowered to a suitable height with the ship's officer and pilot on it.

Plans and specifications of this equipment have been sent by the manufacturers to the authorities concerned for approval and it is confidently expected that it will receive their approval.

Safety is of such importance to pilots that the Recommendations on Performance Standards for Mechanical Pilot Hoists, as signed in November, 1974, are quoted in Appendix G, while a proposal to amend Regulation 17, Chapter V of the 1960 Safety Convention covering pilot ladders and mechanical pilot hoists is given in Appendix H.

A problem which continues to concern pilots is the unusual design features in certain ships in use or being built. Some of these vessels have inward sloping sides resulting in pilot ladders not being secured in a position so that each step rests firmly against the ship's side. This is a requirement of the Safety of Life at Sea (SOLAS) Convention of 1960 and 1974, although there is a provision for special arrangements to be made to the satisfaction of the Administration, but those which have been tried for certain vessels have not proved satisfactory and have endangered the lives of the pilots and the crews of the pilot boats.

Between 1st and 8th March, 1975 the U.K. Pilots' Association engaged in a world-wide Safety Week Campaign under the auspices of the International Maritime Pilots'

Association (I.M.P.A.), the object being to reduce the number of incidents resulting in pilots' deaths and serious injuries due to faulty equipment. Pilots were asked, during that week, to complete a questionnaire noting any defects in pilot ladders and hoists provided for their use when boarding vessels.

The results showed an unsatisfactory state of affairs and are being brought to the attention of I.M.C.O. with the urgent request that naval architects, shipowners and those concerned with the design of new vessels ensure that provision of a safe means of embarking and disembarking pilots be made at an early point in the design stage and not after a major part of construction has been completed.

Welin Pilot Platform System.   Photographed in *The Pilot*, July, 1976

CHAPTER ELEVEN

Ship Handling

WHEN a pilot goes aboard the master invariably gives the charge of navigating the ship to him and nothing should compromise the pilot's control of the navigation.

His first duty, once he knows which ship he is taking, is to obtain details about her draught, destination and, if an inward-bound vessel, to which berth she is bound. He must also procure information about the movements of other ships in the vicinity; weather conditions and the nature of the ship herself can be considered while proceeding in the pilot cutter.

By the time he has climbed the pilot ladder and reached the bridge he will know whether the ship is diesel or turbine-powered. He will assess the manoeuvrability of the vessel and his first few orders to the helmsman should reveal something of the man's ability and knowledge of English. The process of handling depends a great deal on the manner and form in which the pilot gives the orders and the speed with which they are comprehended and executed.

The inward pilot's task is to convert sea navigation into coastal and river or port navigation. In the Thames, Schelde and the Elbe, this is a gradual process but in Milford Haven, Rotterdam and Le Havre, the change is abrupt. The pilot will adjust the speed of the vessel to suit conditions and the time of arrival and will continue to do this as the particular circumstances require. Problems can arise not only with the sudden increase in speed but also if it is abruptly decreased. If the tide is ebbing a pilot will have to know the rate at which it is falling, what the draught is, whether the screw of the vessel is right-hand or left-hand, her handling and steering capabilities, whether the steering is hydraulic or electric hydraulic.

There are certain things which a pilot must be prepared to cope with as they arise and which he cannot foresee. Some are due to natural causes, such as strong tides and winds which affect the steering; some are the result of the condition of the vessel; there may be a fault in the steering gear which affects a stern movement of the ship at a critical moment. One of the greatest fears of pilots is that there may be mechanical faults on the ships they are to handle.

"There is nothing so awful as coming up to a wharf and giving the order to put the ship astern and she is not going to work," says one pilot, adding, "if you knock a ship about that is bad, but if you damage a wharf . . ."

If visibility is poor the pilot must decide whether it is too bad to risk proceeding. He should ensure when he has ordered a course to be steered that the officer of the watch is checking that the order has been correctly carried out. One pilot was severely reprimanded after an accident because, although he had given a correct course, his order was not carried out, the ruling being that he should have asked the master or officer to verify that the correct course was being steered.

When ship handling a pilot has to be very fast in making judgments and taking decisions because it may take a long time for something to happen in response to his order. There is always a lag in time before the steering can be adjusted, or the engine slowed down. In the case of canals it is sometimes necessary to commence slowing down for a lock when it is not less than two miles distant.

The pilot has to be familiar with all the electronic aids on the bridge while radar and fixed shore stations occupy a supporting role. The efficiency of any ship operation, particularly in restricted waters, varies directly with the efficiency of communications, with shore authorities, navigational aid facilities and the ship-to-ship communication. The pilot acts as an essential link in what is a combined operation.

At the U.K.P.A. Annual Conference on 23rd and 24th November, 1971, the President, the Rt Hon James Callaghan, M.P., said, with reference to the Dover Straits:

"The fact that there have been, mercifully, no incidents that have reached the headlines during the last three months does not mean the danger has been averted. All it means is that we have had rather a lucky period." He said that he wanted it to go on record, on behalf of all pilots, that artificial aids such as radar and fixed shore stations were invaluable but they had always to be regarded as playing a supporting role to a pilot on board. "They cannot be a substitute for that pilot. In our view the standard of navigation and seamanship aboard a number of ships is lamentable." He concluded: "What is needed is an extension of the pilotage service and not a substituting of it by artificial aids."

In recent years pilots have been considering the question of ships' bridges, many of which have been designed principally for open water conditions, pilots' particular

Pilot cutter with a pilot's dory—The Hook of Holland.   *Royal Netherlands Navy*

The bridge of a pilot cutter showing the pilot who is about to board a ship checking the position and near traffic on the cutter's radar with the officer of the watch.   *D. A. McDonald*

requirements not being taken into consideration, especially when navigating in restricted waters. They have taken steps to bring their influence to bear on shipowners and naval architects in the design of purpose-built bridges permitting pilots' requirements to be recognised.

In general once a decision is made a pilot should adhere to it, although there are occasions when it has been proved that an unwise judgment about the best method of berthing a large ship has meant a delay of an hour because the pilot should have been aware earlier that his first thinking was mistaken. A good ship handler should have confidence in his ability, initiative, clear thinking, sound judgment and have an alert attitude.

In Port Adelaide, South Australia, the master of a ship having a gross tonnage of or exceeding 100 tons arriving at or off any port where pilotage is compulsory, must receive on board the ship the first pilot who offers himself and demands to conduct the ship into the port. The master of any such ship must not proceed to sea from, or quit his station, or anchorage in any such port without receiving on board a qualified pilot. Any master who contravenes these requirements is guilty of an offence and liable to a penalty not exceeding $500.

The Pilot of July 1972 quotes a lecture given at the 1972 Liverpool Polytechnic seminar by Mr John Farmer, in which he refers to shiphandling in the creek ports of Nigeria. He said that these ports had a special significance because they were the only ports he knew where the master took an active part in the actual shiphandling, adding:

"It seemed to develop into a joint effort between the master and pilot in some of the berths in that region, the head and stern ropes of the ship were secured to the trees at the side of the bush, so it was all rather primitive. Most ships had their own special pilots, but if you had not indicated your choice in advance, then, as you approached the Escravos pilot station, out would streak half a dozen canoes each carrying a pilot and generally the first man to reach the bridge, invariably clutching a wad of references, was given the job. I had a tremendous respect for these pilots who did a marvellous job without the aids we have come to expect as commonplace today. It was in that territory I started to do a little of my own shiphandling and, although I was very proud of my efforts, I realise now how amateurish they were and I will never forget getting myself into a complete 'fankle' on the outskirts of Sapele with eight shackles out on the starboard anchor, my bow in the back garden of the house of a timber exporter, and the second mate from aft telling me to go ahead or our propeller would be in the middle of a log raft being floated upstream. We escaped unscathed and later, when I had recovered, I was pleased I had the experience to relate to other masters trading to that country who always had an equally harrowing tale to tell me whenever we met ashore."

A good pilot knows the feel of a ship. One ship may be said to "handle like a tugboat", and another will be a "clumsy cow".

Pilots identify wholly with every ship they serve; the ship's interest becomes their interest, and safe navigation by pilots is now largely taken for granted. With a full gale it may be questionable whether a pilot can get aboard a vessel; he might be risking his neck to try, yet he will be the man who is working his hardest to get aboard.

R. H. B. Ardley has made a comprehensive survey of ship handling in his book— *Harbour Pilotage.* On emergency measures he has this to say:

"There are occasions when it is necessary, for various reasons, to berth and unmoor ships under conditions which involve considerable hazard of damage. The pilot's stand-by in almost every emergency are the ship's anchors. The old sea maxim—'Never go ashore with an anchor at your bow' may well be altered for narrow waters to 'Never do damage with an anchor at your bow.'. . . If danger of doing damage to other ships or dock construction is imminent, there is one effective remedy at hand. Both anchors are let go, together and on the run, and the cables are allowed to run out until the anchors are able to get an effective grip, when they are checked, and alternately held and grudgingly veered as the ship's way is reduced. It is astonishing how rapidly a ship can be brought up, even if she has good headway, when both anchors are used. If only one is dropped, only half the checking action is exerted, and if an excessive strain is brought on the single cable, it will part or the hawsepipe will split. A ship's windlass is very strongly secured to the deck, and with the cables growing sharply astern a great deal of the stress which would normally come on the windlass is borne at the elbow at the lower end of the hawsepipe. When the stress is carried by both cables and pipes the advantage is clear, and many a ship which has carried away her cable in an emergency and then forged ahead to do damage would today have a clean record if both anchors had been let go."

Deep ships with only two or three feet clearance below the keel require a good deal of

Control Console in the wheelhouse of Cunard Brocklebank's cargo liner mv *Mahout*.

Cunard Steam Ship Company

skill and knowledge, giving little margin for being out of position, as do the super tankers, where the capital cost of the equipment can be as much as £20,000,000, and an hour's delay by making an incorrect decision on the best way to berth the vessel may cost the shipowner an additional £1,000.

In the book just referred to, Ardley writes:

"Ship handling is a fascinating craft—perhaps the most absorbing of all the activities of a seafarer. To stand on the bridge of a fine ship and feel the power of several thousand horses leap to thrashing action at the tinkling of a bell, slewing the ship neatly into her appointed berth, is an unfailingly pleasurable experience. The execution of a slick and safe job in a strong wind or an awkward waterway produces a sense of professional satisfaction at least equal to that enjoyed by any other craftsman."

Some pilots have found that as little as two weeks away from piloting can take a slight edge off their judgment. How much more difficult it is, therefore, for a shipmaster approaching port after perhaps many days on the open sea, to orientate himself to the narrowed perspective of a harbour.

Pilots stress the importance of rest periods but these are very erratic; when the district is busy there is less time off between services. Much of the work is done at night and even when he is at home on call the pilot may be worrying about the kind of ship he will have next. It could be a big modern ship with highly sophisticated equipment, or one in absolute contrast with few aids.

Unsocial hours tend to disrupt family life and can cause a certain amount of frustration and even friction in the home. Yet the fitness of the average pilot is dependent on his having a suitable amount of rest and relaxation from strain between services.

Mr Hignett, in his report on his visits to pilot stations in other countries, writes about this problem of rest periods:

"The exact amount of rest must be dependent on the length and intensity of the previous service. The determination of length of a service must be a balance between physical length (distance) and intensity (density of traffic and/or hazard). It is also a factor that the length (duration) of a pilot's service is not only dependent on mileage but on the average speed possible in the district. This is bound to vary, possibly from day to day, but when considering the work of a pilot the length/intensity of passage under the worst possible circumstances must be a major factor to be taken into account.

It is frequently the case that the pilot has the greatest intensity of work at or near the end of each service, particularly when inward bound, although outward bound there can be a queue of ships for disembarkation of the pilots. The longer the service the more strain arises in berthing or mooring at the end of the passage . . . and tiredness affects judgment.

A reasonable time between services or periods of duty is, therefore, a safety factor in the movement of vessels in Pilot Districts. The service must be held to a reasonable period consistent with traffic density/intensity or work in the manoeuvring areas. But it is noticeable in practice that the duration of the rest period varies inversely with the intensity of service, e.g., when the district is busy there is less time off between services."

Mr Hignett pointed out that the Welland Canal was the only area visited where the pilot had a guaranteed amount of time between services. Here the pilot is granted two hours for travelling time after work, two hours for recreation, eight hours for sleep, plus a further two hours for travel to the next service, a total of fourteen hours.

He adds that even this period proved insufficient when traffic was at its busiest as passages were of eleven to twelve hours duration due to congestion. This resulted in increasing the sick leave in consequence of which some pilots, to help ease the work load, took less than their entitlement of time off, thereby increasing the strain on them.

It has to be remembered that Welland Canal pilots are salaried. Those who are self-employed would doubtless find it a financial strain to take too long a break between servicing ships, or the amount paid by shipowners would have to be increased.

United Kingdom pilots earn between £3,000 and £4,000 a year but some can earn as much as £8,500 depending on the size of the port.

With the high incidence of deaths from heart disease among pilots between thirty-five and fifty years of age, especially since 1962, being three times the national average, a Human Factor Study has been started in an endeavour to assess the position and seek to understand the cause of this and give guide lines and recommendations for the alleviation of such problems as are found to exist.

Research carried out so far seems to suggest that, in addition to the necessity for longer rest periods, the stress caused by increased tension on the bridge, with bigger ships, may have some bearing on this.

A survey revealed that the health of those entering the service is above the national average, which is probably accounted for by the fact that candidates have to undergo a stringent medical examination.

In spite of all the tensions and frequent dangerous situations pilots enjoy their work. Mark Twain's words would be echoed today by most pilots:

"If I have seemed to love my profession, it is no surprising thing for I have loved the profession more than any I have followed."

That sentiment, however, does not prevent pilots from doing everything possible to ensure greater safety measures being provided by shipowners, or preclude the men from their endeavour to improve pensions for themselves and particularly for pilots' widows. There is now a Pilots' National Pension Fund which should remove the anxiety.

The bridge of ms *Borgen*, Passenger/Cargo Ferry, Norway/Newcastle and Harwich, Norway/Denmark.
Fred Olsen Lines

CHAPTER TWELVE

War-Time Pilotage

PILOTS have always played their part in wartime, thought not necessarily in their own district.

At the very commencement of the First World War (1914-1918) the pilotage service in the Isle of Wight district was put under the direct control of the Chief Naval Transport Officer, all orders being treated with the utmost secrecy. Regular liners were piloted out of Southampton, some to go to Liverpool. As soon as they had gone transport ships began to arrive in such numbers that pilots were bringing in and taking out three ships at a time, with one pilot in the leading vessel. There was little time for rest between services, so many ships being required to embark the Expeditionary Force on their way to the war zone.

An area between Horse Sand Fort off Southsea to No Man's Land Fort off Seaview, Isle of Wight, came to be known as the Eastern Gateway, with two Government ships moored head and stern between the two Forts. All ships had to wait for the signal "all's well" before they were allowed to enter or leave this area. Other places around the South Coast were similarly controlled. Many times pilots, having transported ships night and day, sometimes doing three trips in twenty-four hours, had to make their way from Sandown Pier to Ryde and thence via Portsmouth to Southampton to get home.

Later in the war the liners came back bearing as many as 3,000 wounded in one ship. When there were no pilot cutters to ship the pilots a large Government tug was used to convey them to the Nab to meet the incoming vessels. On a few occasions, when neither cutters nor tugs were available to bring pilots back to their home port, they were carried on to the ship's destination which could be as far as New York. Prisoners of war, passengers and crews from captured German ships, service personnel coming on leave or being transferred to another war zone, all had to be piloted in.

There were casualties on both sides. The wreck of one Greek ship sunk during that war is still near the Needles. Pilots were very much in the front line, always there was risk of being attacked by enemy ships, torpedoed, blown up by mines or being at the receiving end of a stick of bombs from a zeppelin.

For more than a month at the end of the war period, when the tug boats were on strike at Southampton, pilots had to handle ships without the aid of tugs. Yet they were tireless in their endeavours to bring ships safely to their destination, often not having time for rest between services, or even a proper meal. If an order came to go they went, regardless of fatigue or danger. It was wartime and pilots, like thousands of others, demonstrated their loyalty in action.

In his book *Pilot Aboard*, John Radford, a Southampton pilot, gives a graphic account of his experiences at that time as he does of the Second World War, in which he also played an important part.

Pilots were again taken over by the Admiralty at the beginning of this War.

At first south coast ports were comparatively quiet and many pilots were transferred to Liverpool and the Clyde. At Dover practically the whole of the station was dispersed. A few pilots joined the Air Force, some went to Iceland. Of those remaining all but two were sent either to the Clyde or to Gravesend. The remaining two stayed in Dover to deal with traffic in Dover Harbour, which was naturally limited at the time, as Dover was under shellfire. The traffic to London Docks was much reduced, most of the American boats using West Coast ports.

In both world wars Liverpool pilots continued to do their business under unusually arduous conditions of enemy activity and black-out. In each of the conflicts cutters were lost with heavy loss of life. John S. Rees, in his *History of the Liverpool Pilotage Service*, relates these two incidents. Of the loss of the *Alfred H. Read* he writes:

"In the early hours of the morning of the 28th December, 1917, the Service suffered one of the greatest disasters that had ever befallen it, when No. 1 pilot boat, the *S.S. Alfred H. Read* struck a mine on the Bar station, sinking in a few minutes, and out of 41 souls on board only two were saved; 19 pilots, 8 apprentices and 12 others making the supreme sacrifice."

Concerning the loss of the other boat Rees writes:

"In the early hours of the morning of Sunday, November 26th, 1939, No. 1 Pilot Boat, the *s.s. Charles Livingston*, stranded on Ainsdale Beach. Shortly afterwards a violent gale from the west-north-west, of hurricane force, developed and heavy seas soon swept away her bridge and upper deck houses.

To prevent being washed overboard, six of her personnel took refuge in the fore-rigging, and were subsequently rescued by the lifeboat, but not before the vessel was completely submerged, with the exception of her masts and the upper part of her funnel. Four others were washed overboard, but were flung on to the beach. All the rest on board, 23 in number, perished, including eight pilots and eight apprentices . . .

A boat having broken adrift with one apprentice in her, two other apprentices, Percy M. Horswell and Frank S. Waddington, put off from the stranded pilot boat in a motor boat, to endeavour to bring her back, but they failed to return.

Two more apprentices, John K. Lancaster and John Tully, then volunteered to make an attempt with another motor boat to rescue their three companions, they also disappeared in the blackness, and all five lost their lives, the tremendous seas overwhelming them.

These gallant deeds were recognised by the Trustees of the Carnegie Hero Fund and certificates to that effect were handed to the parents of the four young men . . .

Eye witnesses have testified to the calmness and great courage displayed by all the apprentices on this disastrous morning."

There was a great influx of shipping to Liverpool during the Second World War, when it became a number one port. Convoys of up to 70 ships arrived with escorts, battle ships,

Liverpool pilot boat *Alfred H. Read* sunk by a mine 1917. Liverpool pilot boat *Charles Livingston* wrecked 1939.
J. Delacour-Keir

cruisers, carriers and troop ships converging on Liverpool, 90 per cent of them taking pilots. Altogether 1,285 convoys arrived in Liverpool during the Second World War, while 75,000,000 tons of cargo, including food, raw materials and supplies, were handled, and 4,750,000 men, 1,250,000 of whom were American, passed through the port.

Two-thirds of the port was either destroyed or severely damaged during the war and the new development culminated in the building of the Royal Seaforth Dock.

During the war there was no night navigation of big ships on the Manchester Ship Canal, which was miraculously saved from damage apart from the bank outside Eastern Lock, which was hit, but the Canal remained operative.

When war was declared in 1939 the Clyde Pilotage Service had an organisation and structure quite unsuited to the requirements of war. Unlike many other pilotage districts pilots did not cruise at sea on a cruising cutter, with sleeping accommodation and catering facilities. Instead the pilots kept watch, four at a time, in the pilot station at the west end of Gourock Pier and went off to ships after they had rounded the Cloch lighthouse. There was a large cutter capable of transporting pilots down to the Cumbrae Heads to meet ships which required a pilot there, but even this larger cutter had sleeping accommodation for only two and had no catering facilities.

Wartime conditions required pilots to meet ships in the vicinity of Ascog near Craigmore, on the island of Bute, and a pilot station at Gourock was quite unable to perform this service. The pilots themselves, therefore, chartered a large boarding house in the vicinity and the supply of pilots to the ships inwards to the Clyde was performed from this house until a large cruising cutter with adequate catering facilities and sleeping accommodation could be provided.

In the course of time, as other ports became more and more vulnerable to air attack, Clyde became the most important base for shipping in the country and Clyde pilots were supplemented by pilots from many other ports in Britain. The pace was hectic, the *Queen Elizabeth* and *Queen Mary* came in regularly and there were a great many troop ships, but Greenock was one of the safest places in the country.

Many large houses were taken over by the Admiralty, which had the task of regulating convoys. The vast majority of cargo ships using the ports were coal burning and had to be bunkered. Some American ships had orders to go to Liverpool but lost their way and had to be piloted to that port. Pilots by their calling, are accustomed to providing a twenty-four hour service for every day of the year. During the war years that condition was never breached and for the pilots concerned the problem was how to get enough sleep to enable them to keep going and how to get a reasonable meal.

"The first night of the war was a memorable time," says Murdoch Mackenzie, a Clyde pilot, for many years retired following a back injury sustained in a fall from a pilot ladder. "We knew that a blitz could be unleashed on us at any time. The navigation lights on the river had to be dimmed so that most of them were out. I was on watch in the pilot station at Gourock when, in the darkness of the firth, a small light blinked: long long short — long long short. 'I want a pilot.'

I went off to her in the cutter, She was a destroyer, the *Vanquisher*. I climbed up to the bridge.

'Pilot, we're going up river to Old Kilpatrick to bunker.'

'We can't do that. Most of the lights are out in the river.'

'Pilot, the *Athenia* has been torpedoed and is sinking. I'm going out to her.'

'Oh,' I said, 'that's different. Half ahead both engines,' and off we went—up river."

During the war the Clyde was the European centre of allied shipping. There were hundreds of ships constantly in the Clyde. It was a day and night non-stop job for the pilots. They piloted ships on the river and on the Firth, round the coasts of Britain mainly to the convoy assembly places.

"The eeriest job of all," says Mackenzie, "was when we went out to sea with tugs to get hold of ships which had been mined or torpedoed and attempted to tow them to shallow water where they could be beached in safety. To stand on the bridge of these ships, watching them gradually sink lower and lower in the water as they were slowly and painfully towed up the Firth—wondering if you would get them safely on to the beach, or whether they would sink under your feet in deep water was an eerie experience.

One of my own jobs during the war was to pilot the *Queen Mary* and the *Queen Elizabeth*. One example shows how difficult it is for a person who has had no training in pilotage to understand the hidden dangers which can afflict a ship when everything seems to be perfectly safe and in order.

I was piloting the *Queen Mary* up towards the narrow gateway in the boom defence, which stretched across from the Cloch to Dunoon, the wind was strong south-west, blowing on the port quarter. When the other pilots saw me coming up with this big ship they kept out of my way and gave me a free passage because they knew that these ships, with their very high superstructure, were very much affected by the wind and had to be kept moving at good speed to enable them to steer properly and keep them under control.

On this occasion, however, dead ahead was a little/little herring drifter, right in the middle of the narrow channel, and I was overtaking him fast.

I ordered all engines dead slow ahead and gave a long blast on the whistle to let him know that I was there. No answer.

I gave him another blast on the whistle to say—'Please move over a bit and give me room to get through the gateway.' No answer.

He was still right in the middle of the narrow channel—dead ahead. The *Queen Mary* was steaming dead slow, she was just steering, the helm was hard-a-starboard to counteract the push of the wind on her port quarters. We were approaching the gateway, and we were overtaking the drifter, fast.

In desperation I ordered—'All engines stop.' I began to sweat.

Almost immediately the *Queen Mary* lost steering-way. The wind pushed her stern to starboard and her bow swung to port, straight for the gate vessel of the boom. I had to make an immediate decision. It was either the gate vessel or the drifter. I chose the drifter and ordered all engines full speed ahead. The helm was hard-a-starboard as the propellers bit, gradually, slowly, the bow of the *Queen Mary* swung away from the gate vessel into the gateway. We cleared the gate vessel and, by amazing good luck, we missed the drifter as well.

We had got away with it, no lives lost, no damage done, just one of those things so common in pilotage.

The next day I happened to pilot a little ship into the Albert Harbour at Greenock and there was the little drifter. Out of curiosity I went on board her. A tall, handsome, bearded man was on deck. I approached him.

'Are you the skipper?' I asked.

'Aye, I am that.'

'I was the pilot on board the *Queen Mary* yesterday,' I said, tentatively.

'Oh,' he said, 'you were the daft man who passed me in the gateway. That was a helleva place to pass another ship.'

'Well,' I said humbly, 'I blew the whistle to ask you to move over a bit to give me room to pass through the gateway.'

He bridled visibly.

'Why should I get out of your way? I had as much right to be there as you had and, in any case, you were going far too fast.'

I retreated—defeated."

As master mariners pilots' work was not confined to the Clyde; they also did a considerable amount of pilotage of ships around the coasts, mainly to other convoy ports such as Liverpool or Oban or Loch Ewe. If a captain was not available for any sort of ship, then a Clyde pilot always was.

By now the original band of Clyde pilots was almost submerged by the wave of Trinity House pilots from London and Southampton who had come north to assist at this busy port. This could only happen in wartime because, although they had the same qualifications and background experience, they were only licensed for their own pilotage district. It is an offence under the Pilotage Act for a pilot to take a ship in a pilotage district not his own.

The work was non-stop, the general plan being the pilotage of ships up the river during the day and piloting convoys at night.

When, eventually the turn of the tide of war came and everything began to build up to D Day, though few knew what that involved at the time, Southampton and London pilots were recalled to their own districts and a number of temporary men were employed as pilots to assist them. On D Day literally hundreds of ships were anchored everywhere around the south coast, while pilots were on duty for twenty-five hours going back and forth across the Channel with amphibious craft filled with men intent on making an end to the war they had endured for so long, or bringing back those already wounded in the landings.

During the post-war years shipyards were re-equipped and passenger ships were built to replace those lost during the war. Overwhelming numbers of Liberty ships built in the United States were available as cargo boats and pilots prepared to engage in their normal pilotage duties.

Pilots going out to be put on various ships in a convoy.   *Sport and General Press Agency Limited*

CHAPTER THIRTEEN

Super Tankers

NO MATTER what the method of transport, by road, rail, air or sea, there is always the desire to go faster in bigger, better, more sophisticated vehicles or craft.

The closing of the Suez Canal on 16th November, 1956 is given as the reason for the greatly increased size of oil tankers. Since the journey had to be extended some means of reducing the cost had to be found. The result was that oil tankers developed into Very Large Crude Carriers, leaping from about 100,000 tons deadweight to 300,000 tons for the long distance crude oil traffic. Tanker speeds, however, have not materially increased, 15/16 knots being the most economic rate.

Although the oil boycott, which started in 1973, halted progress and reduced the number of tankers in transit, oil companies continued to look ahead, regarding this as only a temporary setback.

Whether or not the Canal had been closed, this explosion in the size of cargo and speed of shipping would doubtless have been forced upon us by economics and advanced engineering technology, although possibly it would not have occurred with quite the same speed.

However advantageous such changes are, they create their own particular problems which, if not recognised and controlled, can more than outweigh the benefits.

The first thing which comes to mind is the possibility of greater risk of accidents, especially in restricted and congested waters where compulsory pilotage does not exist. Following a number of serious collisions in the Dover Straits, I.M.C.O. produced a traffic separation scheme and ships in the 300 separation zones in operation throughout the world were asked to observe the rule of the road and keep to their separate sea lanes, but this cannot be enforced.

While it is claimed that these very large vessels have created no insurmountable problems for their pilots, and the handling characteristics are as good, if not better than small sized ships, they agree that manoeuvrability in stopping distances and turning circle need greater consideration.

The highly responsible task of bringing in these super tankers, with 300 ships a day passing back and forth in the restricted waters of the Dover Straits, can be appreciated when one remembers that they are a quarter of a mile in length and 170 feet in breadth and are approximately as high from the normal deck as a six storey block of flats with as much of the ship under the water as above. Some are even larger and their stopping distance is 12 miles after the change from full speed ahead. In the event of emergency, however, stopping distance can be brought down to 2½ miles in restricted waters while in unrestricted waters avoiding action can be taken by turning full circle. These tankers are, in fact, claimed to be the largest moving objects built by man.

With their long experience of ship handling and complete familiarity with the confined waters of their own district, pilots are well able to handle these, though problems can arise where there is lack of room for manoeuvre on account of the depth and width of the channel and when other ships fail to observe the rule of the road. Pilots are very conscious of the vulnerability of the cargo carried, while the Torrey Canyon Disaster alerted the public to the risks and gave further emphasis to pilots' campaign for compulsory pilotage.

Berthing such huge vessels has presented its own problems, which is one reason why only experienced senior pilots handle vessels over a certain tonnage.

Most pilots think that dual pilotage is necessary on these large ships. In European Maritime Pilots' Association countries, where dual pilotage is normal, this appears to work quite satisfactorily and is considered essential for very large ships. Even in Germany, where pilotage is non-compulsory, masters never refuse the offer of a second pilot or even, in some cases, three, with full dues being paid for each pilot.

At a recent Annual General Meeting of E.M.P.A., after discussion of this question, a resolution was passed unanimously that:

"It should be made compulsory for ships of exceptional dimensions to employ more than one pilot, the additional number of pilots being decided by the navigational conditions in the port and its approaches."

Yet, in spite of reduced crews and many being less efficient and unable to steer well because they have become so accustomed to automatic steering, most shipping companies are against the employment of more than one pilot, being unwilling to pay for the additional service.

Not only is there the question of length and breadth of these tankers but there is the problem of under keel clearance in harbours which were never intended for vessels of such size and where wharves and jetties were constructed with smaller ships in mind.

In January 1974 a conference was held in the United Kingdom on Ship Behaviour in Confined Waters, its objective being to bring together representatives of research organisations, shipping interests and the port industry to present the conclusions of recent research into the behaviour of ships in confined waters and to provide a forum for the exchange of views between those engaged in research and those expected to apply the research results to the practicalities of port and shipping. The Conference was sponsored by The Chamber of Shipping of the United Kingdom, the National Ports Council and The National Physical Laboratory, and was opened by Dr I. Maddock, Chief Scientist of the Department of Trade.

Glasgow University had already undertaken research into this important subject both in model tank tests and on board a 200,000 ton tanker on regular voyage in the loaded condition from the Persian Gulf to Rotterdam, also on three other large tankers. One thing which was particularly noticeable was that when the ship's speed was reduced to nine knots to allow the arrival and departure of the helicopter used to transfer the pilot from the shore to the ship, as the speed decreased the trim changed from by the head to trim by the stern, in other words, when the speed decreases there is a corresponding rise of the bow.

In a paper prepared for The Chamber of Shipping in the United Kingdom, A. M.

Getting a large ship through a small hole. Soviet Training Ship *Professor Rybaltovski* being piloted out of Dover's Granville Dock by a Cinque Ports' Pilot.

D. A. McDonald

Ferguson, in charge of research into squat at Glasgow University, summarised the position as follows:

"One of several reactions which every ship experiences when moving through calm water is a change in vertical position relative to the undisturbed sea surface. This reaction is normally accompanied by a change in longitudinal trim. It is the combination of these reactions which is referred to as squat, meaning a lowering of position relative to the surface.

Increasing speed and decreasing under-keel clearance are the two main factors which cause an increase in squat. It is this second factor, shallow water, which has assumed an increasing importance in recent years. For economic reasons, the trend to increase the size of oil and bulk carriers has continued. with vessels of one million tons dw envisaged. For these very large ships, with draughts of 20 to 30 metres, large areas of the North Sea and English Channel now present shallow water conditions.

From model tests conducted at Glasgow University over the period 1965 to 1969, it was apparent that accurate knowledge of squat in shallow water is essential for the safe navigation of very large ships and a programme of shallow water experiments was therefore devised and carried out."

Further research is necessary before any firm conclusions can be arrived at.

Milford Haven was one of the first ports in the United Kingdom to handle these large tankers. A certain amount of blasting had to be done, corners were knocked off the rock bottom and the entrance deepened slightly. Tankers come in fully laden drawing 67 feet draught. A Harbour Surveillance System was installed and the communications system was modernised, while plans were made for a Channel Approach Aid System to assist pilots and masters in manoeuvring individual ships. In addition to the radar installed in the Milford Haven Conservancy Board's Signal Station, two Coastguard radars are connected by microwave links to the display console in the Signal Station. These three radars provide complete coverage of the Haven and its approaches with rapid and accurate fixing of vessels in the main channels. This assists in programming shipping by providing piloted and unpiloted vessels with information of the position of other ships so that they do not meet in the congested parts of the Haven or at the West Angle Buoy entrance.

All pilots and ship masters are asked to report to the Signal Station by radio telephone, giving details of their shipping movements to enable this service to become fully operative. Remedial action as necessary is the responsibility of those handling the vessels.

Rotterdam can now take roughly the same draught but dredgers have to be kept going twenty-four hours a day because of the dirt and sand suspended in the water causing silting. One V.L.C.C. had to be brought back to Milford Haven from Rotterdam to lighten the load before she could be berthed at that port.

It has now become a common practice to lighten some tankers to enable them to enter certain ports such as Fawley, where 47 feet is the maximum draught which can be accommodated.

Loch Long jetties, at Finnart (Clydeport) have been found so suitable for berthing the largest size oil tankers that ships too deep draughted to enter some of the major ports are calling there to discharge part of their cargo before proceeding to their destination.

On 15th January, 1972 the Liberian oil tanker *Universe Kuwait*, then the third largest ship in the world, came up the Clyde to discharge part of her cargo of 325,000 tons of oil at Finnart, which is only one of two ports in North West Europe deep enough to take a vessel 1,132 feet long, 175 feet beam, with a draught of 82 feet. Finnart is the only terminal in Europe linked to a refinery which could take this vessel when fully laden.

Clydeport Authority discovered it was necessary to find locations suited to the individual needs of these tankers. One prospective oil company required a deep water jetty in the Firth only for the discharge of crude oil to be pumped to a refinery fourteen miles away adjacent to the Clyde from which the refined product could be exported. In this particular instance flat land near the deep water berth was not required. An oil jetty was, therefore, planned for Wemyss Point, near Greenock, similar to those already established at Finnart on Loch Long by the British Petroleum Company. These jetties are used only for the discharge of crude oil, this being pumped right across Scotland to the refinery at Grangemouth.

Another jetty was planned for the deep water of Portincross and the refinery adjacent to it on the southern point of the Hunterston promontory. This was done to suit the requirements of an oil company which did require flat land close to a berth. Normally it would be preferable to build jetties in well-sheltered areas, but V.L.C.C.'s are different from other vessels in that they neither pitch nor roll and the seas break helplessly against them. Once the oil has been pumped out of them the tanks can be filled with sea-water to act as ballast to maintain them in deep draught condition.

Rotterdam had, at an early time, developed into one of the most important oil importing centres on the Continent. A large storage site had been constructed on the South Bank at a safe distance from harbours for dry cargo ships, but the steady growth of the port brought the two sections too near to each other. It was, therefore, decided to remove the industry to a site lower down the river with an area of 1,300 acres on which two harbours were planned, the 1st and 2nd Petroleum Harbour.

Further extension of the port was realised in the Europort project, which has an open connection with the North Sea. To make the Europort harbours and the harbour and industrial area on the Maasvlakte, which is in course of development, accessible for the largest tankers and bulk carriers, a fairway was dredged with a length of 16 miles into the North Sea for ships with a draught of 68 feet and 300,000 tons dw, as explained previously. Yet even this is not adequate for the super tankers, and Europort is unable to take the largest tankers until they are lightened. Buoys are established in deep water with pipelines laid across the sea and tankers can tie up with these buoys without going close to a port.

When a master takes a new ship he goes to every part of it to make sure he can hear the alarm. If he cannot hear it anywhere the oil company will put in another. The crew numbers about 40 and there is so much instrumentation that the tendency is for the engagement of still smaller crews. In fact, the crew on a super tanker, with its automatic steering, is often less than that necessary on older and smaller tankers.

Engine rooms are always at the bottom of the ship, but many ships have bridge engine control.

The engine room can be unmanned because of the high degree of computerisation. Engineers can be called by the computer when there is an indication that something may be going wrong. The alarm will continue to sound until the call is accepted when the engineer reaches the engine room. If for any reason it does not stop, a light flashes in the officers' mess. The fault is automatically printed on a continuous roll of paper in a machine in the engine room as it occurs, with the date and the time the fault occurred. If it has corrected itself, as frequently happens, this will also have been recorded automatically but the engineer will still check.

On a fine day a fault may be purposely injected into the system to test it. Everything automatically slows down until it has been corrected, when it automatically starts up again.

Much of the equipment is duplicated and in the event of a breakdown the alternative equipment automatically takes over. In the engine room everything is duplicated, even the control pump for pumping out the oil.

There is direct communication by radio telephone to the London office from almost any part of the world.

While there is natural concern among the public regarding the risk of accidents to these enormous tankers, it is surprising to learn that there have been fewer collisions and consequences of faulty navigation than with smaller vessels. That this does not always seem to be the case is probably accounted for by the news value of such incidents as do occur to V.L.C.C.'s and other bulk carriers, especially considering the serious consequences of any spillage of oil or explosion of chemical products.

Shell Appropriated Pilot, J. MacKay, taking *Berge Bergesen* to Tranmere, 1967.

Mersey Docks and Harbour Company

CHAPTER FOURTEEN

What of the Future?

WHEN Queen Elizabeth I, speaking of the freedom of the seas said, "the use of the sea is common to all, neither may any title to the ocean belong to any people or private man," ships were smaller, less costly to run and time was not such an important factor as it has become today.

Even so, with masters and ship owners regarding freedom of the seas as their right, there were many groundings, or strandings, with much loss of life and cargo. Today, especially with potentially dangerous chemicals and oil conveyed in mammoth ships, most smaller vessels tend to make way for bulk carriers and large tankers. Trouble ensues with those who, in their desire to reach their destination on time, fail to consider the inherent dangers of, for instance, crossing the sea lanes in order to save a tide.

The figures of ship losses for 1971 round the coasts of the United Kingdom reflect the need for pilots. In that year 377 vessels were lost, the highest ever recorded for any year other than during war-time. Of the 1,000,000 gross tons represented by these ships lost, 27,000 tons were British. At one period there were 14 wreck buoys and 2 wreck warning light vessels marking the wrecks in one wreck area yet, despite all these devices, crews of the light vessels had to spend a good deal of time warning ships away by using Aldis lamps and sound and trace rockets.

With electronic devices replacing equipment previously operated manually, it is all too easy for ships' officers to become instrument conscious and less practical in their seamanship. Small wonder, therefore, that all large tankers take pilots.

Most pilotage authorities have a very good record of safety with ships which have been piloted between the ocean and the quayside. The Port of Brisbane, for example, claims to have a world-wide reputation for skill and safety. Their performance book reads: "In 125 years of service (since Queensland became a State) not a single ship, or life, has been lost while a pilot has had charge of a vessel within the Port limits."

Both the size of ships and the character of the cargoes conveyed in them have completely changed since the Pilotage Act was passed over sixty years ago, but there has been very little legislation since that date to prevent these being moved in pilotage waters without the aid of a pilot. Lives, ships and even dock areas are thus exposed to unnecessary hazards from noxious and dangerous cargoes. A major spillage of certain cargo resulting from an error in navigation or a collision with another vessel, can affect the ecology of a whole region to say nothing of the risk to life involved.

What changes, therefore, can we expect in the next sixty years? As an indication of the type of shipping envisaged for the future, Mr J. M. Farmer, Gourock pilot, reminded an audience of pilots a few years ago that "delegates to a conference in the United States of

America were asked to discuss the form of international control required within 20 years when 100-knot nuclear-powered, unmanned vessels were sailing the North Atlantic."

One pilot, in an article in *The Pilot* of September, 1971, discussed the possibilities of what could be achieved using available techniques:—

"'Hands off' in the engine room is already a working proposition, although standby is usually adopted during manoeuvring. 'Hands off' in navigation is also possible if radar can be relied upon to supplant the human eye to avoid collision. Automatic course holding by compass, radio navigator, inertial guidance and astro-navigation are all well tried and fully engineered achievements. It needs only a small sized crystal ball and a little imagination to postulate the future methods of the bulk oil traffic, subject to progressive acceptance of the ideas by Lloyds and other interested maritime authorities.

The crystal ball picture is far from obscure. It clearly portrays tankers of 500,000 dwt and upwards leaving a middle eastern loading berth with a small crew and where appropriate, a pilot. On reaching open sea and headed on her course, the ship is put on full auto-control with a complete course programme set in the computer. The entire crew then leaves by helicopter to pick up an incoming ship or to return to their middle eastern base.

The unmanned tanker will proceed round the Cape, through the Bay of Biscay until, just off Brest, a pilot and skeleton crew will join her by helicopter and take her to Milford Haven, or through the Channel to Rotterdam, or wherever else the orders require.

It is foreseeably no less safe to herself or to other shipping than a conventionally manned tanker. It may well be cheaper to operate in the unmanned condition except at the ends of each voyage and the living pattern for crews would be significantly improved. In European territorial waters and their approaches, the services of pilots could well be in greater demand than hitherto, and with scope for greater responsibility. One might stretch the imagination a little further and suggest that, apart from emergency repairs, only a pilot is needed to berth or to take out an auto-controlled vessel, thus dispensing with the conventional concept of a 'resident' crew altogether."

Another pilot's estimate of the effect on pilots of the changes taking place in the maritime world was that pilots and the pilotage service will play an increasingly important, integrated role in a fully integrated transport industry. They will become the specialist link between the ocean and the quayside.

Let us hope that if and when such a time comes, these ships will be subject to compulsory pilotage although, as Mr Rhodes remarked, "this will be placing a very much greater strain and responsibility on the pilot who is taking over the ship for mooring, unmooring, navigating in confined waters and with a need to control the ship and her attendant tugs."

A quote from an article by Mr Frank Berry, Vice President of the U.K.P.A. and Chairman of the Executive Committee, himself a Humber pilot, aptly sums up the situation:

"Without a doubt the need for the services of a pilot will be questioned again when the fully computerised shiphandling techniques are developed but, somehow, I feel pilots are going to be around for a long time yet."

Shell tanker ss *Latirus*.
A Shell Photograph

Appendix A

MARINE PILOTAGE

A POLICY STATEMENT
Department of Trade, London
1975

1. It has been recognised for some years now that the Pilotage Act 1913, is out of date and discussions with the various interests concerned with marine pilotage on the changes needed have taken place over a considerable period. In particular, the Steering Committee on Pilotage, appointed in September 1973, examined the subject in detail and, in the summer of 1974, presented a unanimous report entitled 'Marine Pilotage in the United Kingdom', published by H.M. Stationery Office.

2. It is unlikely that legislative time can be made available in the current Parliamentary Session for a new Bill to supersede the Pilotage Act, 1913. Nevertheless, the Government attaches importance to bringing about as soon as possible changes in the pilotage system to accord with modern requirements. In order to remove uncertainty and to encourage some planning to proceed in advance of new legislation, the Government is issuing this policy statement. In addition to commenting on and in general accepting the recommendations made in the Steering Committee's report, reference is made in paragraph 11 to developments which may be possible, after consultation with the interests concerned, in advance of new legislation.

3. The summary of main findings and recommendations contained in Chapter 1 of the Steering Committee's report is reproduced as an annex to this statement. The principal aims are safety in changing conditions, improved organisation of the system and fair treatment of the pilots themselves and, while some recommendations would contribute to a number of these aims, it is convenient to consider them in these three groups.

Safety

4. Recommendations in the first group are designed to ensure that pilotage continues to keep pace with modern conditions of ships and marine traffic. This includes recommendations on the relationship of the pilot to the master (Recs 1 and 2), selective pilotage systems (Rec 3), qualifications, training and mobility (Recs 6 and 7), and assistants to the pilots of certain ships (Rec 13). Perhaps the most important aspect, however, is the combination of compulsory pilotage in major ports as a general principle (Rec 8) and supplementary arrangements making it compulsory to take a pilot in cases of special risk (Rec 11) with a liberal attitude towards the issue, without automatic restriction to British subjects, of pilotage certificates to masters of chief officers of ships which use a port frequently and can demonstrate their familiarity with it by examination (Rec 9 and Rec 12).

5. The Government accepts these recommendations and believes that taken as a whole they will contribute to maritime safety and avoidance of pollution. It considers that responsibility for the statutory survey of pilot craft, as distinct from management and advice on such craft, should rest with the Department of Trade (Rec 29).

Organisation

6. The second group of recommendations is designed to produce a more representative management structure and one more responsive to change. In major ports and estuaries, there would be local pilotage authorities representative of shipowners, pilots and ports with independent members contributing additional navigational and management experience (Rec 17) and the areas covered by such authorities would allow a single pilot to pilot a ship from the seaward boundary to its berth and vice versa subject to considerations of fatigue and expertise (Rec 18). There would be a Central Board appointed by the Secretary of State composed of similar interests to carry out work best handled centrally and to take the lead in reorganising the system (Recs 19 and 20).

7. The Government accepts these recommendations but considers also that, without prejudice to the general policy of devolution of functions, the Central Board should be required to consult a special Committee of Scottish interests on matters concerning pilotage in Scotland. Details of the membership and standing of this Committee will be discussed along with the constitution of the Board. Consideration is also being given to suitable arrangements for consulting Welsh interests. While the Government recognises the special problems of smaller ports it does not, at this stage, wish to take a view on the alternative methods of relating smaller ports to the new organisations arrangements referred to in recommendation 21 and thinks it likely that this should await the setting up of a Central Board. There is a separate reference below to Trinity House, London.

Fair Treatment of Pilots

8. The third group of recommendations is concerned with fair conditions of employment and remuneration of the pilots themselves. The Government accepts that self-employment should continue at least until it is possible to judge whether the organisational changes secure the benefits expected but that legislation should not preclude employment on a salaried basis (Rec 4). It also accepts that the Central Board should seek to secure equitable staffing and remuneration, that there should be arrangements to help compensate pilots for temporary losses of earnings outside their control (Rec 5) and that legislative provision should be made for compensation in the event of redundancy (Rec 27). The recommendations regarding more stringent requirements for communicating time of arrival (Rec 10), regarding the basis of pilotage dues (Recs 14 and 15) and penalties for the late payment of dues (Rec 16) are also accepted: and it is also agreed that ships carrying certificated masters should meet a proportion of pilotage dues (Rec 9). Pilotage is an exacting calling and the Government believes it important that the conditions under which pilots operate should be such as to motivate them to give of their best.

Trinity House, London

9. The Government has noted that under the recommendations in the Steering Committee report Trinity House London would no longer be a pilotage authority for the larger ports but would continue to provide a source of independent navigational advice at local and national level (Rec 22) and would probably continue to have a special responsibility for a number of smaller ports. The Government is mindful of the great traditions and experience of Trinity House in this field and the initiative it has taken, of which one example is its important role in setting up the Pilots' National Pension Fund; and it intends that this experience and the contribution it can make should be fully taken into account in working out details of the new arrangements. There is also the point that during the transition period from the existing to the new arrangements, Trinity House will need to continue with its existing responsibilities as well as playing a part in the introduction of the new system. This should be borne in mind in connection with the recommendation that its pilotage staff should be absorbed into the new system (Rec 23) but it is hoped that any difficulties in this respect may be overcome. The Government also notes the generous offer of Trinity House to house the Central Board but considers that its permanent home will be a matter for the Board itself which may wish to take account of any proposals which emerge for dispersing the work of Government Departments with which they will be most closely associated. The Government also hopes that the title Trinity House Pilot will be preserved at least for pilots previously qualified as such.

Other Recommendations

10. The remaining recommendations in the report deal with provisional licences (Rec 24) which is accepted; with pilotage to the berth (Rec 25) and River Thames pilotage (Rec 26) which call for discussion with local interests; and with up-dating penalties (Rec 28) which is accepted.

Developments in Advance of Legislation

11. While many of the recommendations in the report must await new legislation, it may be possible, given the goodwill which exists, to make limited progress on such matters as pilot qualifications, compulsory pilotage and pilotage certificates. This might take the form of promoting new subordinate legislation under the 1913 Act. The Government will also examine, with interested parties, what action might be taken in advance of a new Act, on remuneration, pensions, training, dues, provisional licences and pilot craft surveys. It is also hoped that discussions which are in progress regarding reorganisation in local pilotage districts will be pressed forward and that other organisational changes which conform with the general policy set out in this statement will be planned. It is recognised, however, that major changes will not be possible until new legislation is passed.

Conclusion

12. The Government believes that these proposals provide a sensible and practical basis for advances in the organisation of pilotage in this country to meet today's requirements and those of the future. These are vastly different from those of 1913. Ships are far larger, draw much more water, and carry dangerous cargoes that could cause serious damage to the environment if they do not enter our ports safely. Great advances have been made in radio and electronic aids to navigation on the basis of which ships now move in states of visibility which in 1913 would have closed a port down. It believes that our pilots are equal to these new problems and that the new framework of legislative and organisational changes set out in this statement will, when implemented, greatly assist them in their important work.

SUMMARY OF MAIN FINDINGS AND RECOMMENDATIONS OF THE REPORT "MARINE PILOTAGE IN THE UNITED KINGDOM"

Relationship of the Pilot to the Master, the Shipowner and the Port (Chapter 3)

While the respective roles of pilot and master are very difficult to define, we reaffirm that the pilot conducts the navigation of the ship while the master retains supreme authority on board and may, where

Rec 1 essential for safety, override the pilot. On balance, we *recommend* against attempting to spell out this

Rec 2 relationship in a new Act. We also *recommend* that the provisions of the 1913 Act regarding the pilot's liability to the shipowner should be left unchanged though it might be desirable to remove the need to

Rec 3 execute a bond. We further *recommend* that selective pilotage should be continued where the parties concerned favour it. While pilotage should, as now, usually be administered independently of the port, there should be the closest co-operation between the two.

Pilots' Remuneration (Chapter 4)

Most pilots value their self-employed status though it has some characteristics of salaried employment.

Rec 4 Advocates of salaried status believe it would achieve greater efficiency and security. We *recommend* against making a change from self-employment but believe that the new legislation should keep open the

Rec 5 possibility in the light of increased efficiency secured by reorganisation. We further *recommend* that central machinery should seek to secure equitable remuneration including application of work indices and that a central fund should help to compensate pilots for losses of earnings outside their control.

Qualifications, Training and Mobility (Chapter 5)

Most pilots are recruited from the merchant service while the remainder come through apprenticeship schemes.

Rec 6 Except for certain small pilotage districts, we *recommend* that a master foreign-going certificate should be the minimum qualification in future, subject to fulfilling obligations to apprentices and perhaps continuation of arrangements for prospective pilots to have an early identification with pilotage. We also

Rec 7 *Recommend, partly to facilitate mobility, a nationally agreed training programme for pilots possibly including simulator training*, with special training in respect of an individual pilotage area.

Compulsory Pilotage and Pilotage Certificates (Chapter 6)

The existing requirements for compulsory pilotage are anachronistic and need review in the light of

Rec 8 present-day risks. We *recommend* that, as a general principle, pilotage should be compulsory subject to carefully considered local exemptions for areas, small vessels and experienced personnel where these can safely be given and certain general exemptions, e.g. in respect of H.M. ships. Linked with this recom-

Rec 9 mendation, we *recommend* a liberal attitude to the issue of pilotage certificates to masters or chief officers of ships which use a port frequently and can demonstrate their familiarity with it by examination; and that

Rec 10 those ships should meet a portion of pilotage costs. We also *recommend more stringent requirements for communicating estimated times of arrival or departure with penalties for infringement*. We further

Rec 11 *recommend* that there should be arrangements *to require a pilot to be taken in cases of special risk*.

Nationality Questions (Chapter 7)

The Pilotage Act places no nationality restrictions on granting pilots' licences but many byelaws restrict them to British subjects. With the exception of certain long-standing ferry services, the Act prohibits the issue of pilotage certificates to aliens. These provisions may need to be considered in the light of E.E.C. obligations; general provisions on nationality matters in a new Pilotage Act might be activated by

Rec 12 Commencement Order. Bearing these questions in mind we *recommend* that the automatic restriction of pilotage certificates to British subjects should be removed though all certificate holders should have fluent command of English and appropriate qualifications. This recommendation is subject to consideration of the effect on demand for pilots and on pilotage finances, measures to ease possible redundancies in certain ports, as well as the scope for reciprocity. We see no special merit in nationality restrictions on pilot licences for which a U.K. master's foreign-going certificate would be required.

Assistant to the Pilot (Chapter 8)

Mainly for very large ships but also in certain very difficult waterways there is a need for a pilot to have an

Rec 13 assistant. We *recommend* that a new Pilotage Act should enable byelaws to be made which would make it compulsory for an assistant to be taken on a vessel for which a need had been established.

Pilotage Dues (Chapter 9)

While there is a good case, supported by practice abroad, for levying a basic charge whether a pilot is taken or not, the need for this may be less in view of the proposed extension of compulsory pilotage

Rec 15 and we *recommend* that a central organisation should review this question. We also *recommend* that the
Rec 15 basis on which pilotage dues are levied should be studied centrally and that charging and accounting
Rec 16 arrangements should be simplified and rationalised. We further *recommend* that a new Act should specify penalties in the event of dues not being paid within a given time.

Future Organisation (Chapter 10)

Larger Ports and Estuaries

More than 1400 of some 1600 U.K. pilots are concerned with piloting vessels into and out of the major ports and estuaries of the U.K. and the organisational solution adopted must ensure an effective and
Rec 17 efficient service. We *recommend* that responsibility and authority be given to local pilotage authorities representative of shipowners, pilots and ports together with some independent members who could
Rec 18 contribute additional navigational and management experience. We further *recommend* that the areas covered by such authorities should allow a single pilot to pilot a ship from the seaward boundary of the district to its berth and vice versa, subject to considerations of fatigue and the required expertise in internal dock systems.

Central Board

Rec 19 We *recommend* that a Central Board be established with specified functions on a continuing basis and the authority to play a part in reorganisation through membership of local reorganisation committees. While its general field of operations should be specified in legislation, flexibility to vary its functions in the light
Rec 20 of experience should be allowed. We *recommend* that the Chairman and Board members should be appointed by the Secretary of State and would include *shipowners, serving pilots, port operators* and *others with a nautical, financial or administrative background.* A full-time staff of perhaps 20-30 would be required.

Smaller Ports

Rec 21 We *recommend* that the possibility of *including smaller ports in larger pilotage districts* nearby or of amalgamating with other smaller districts should be considered. Alternatively, the Central Board might have a small ports section or some small ports might continue with their present administration for some time to come.

Future Role of Trinity House London

Rec 22 While Trinity House itself would cease to be a pilotage authority for larger ports we *recommend* that it should continue to provide a source of independent navigational advice at local and national level which has proved of great value in the past. It would probably have a special responsibility for a number of
Rec 23 smaller ports. We also *recommend* that its pilotage staff should be absorbed into the new system, that the Central Board should be housed initially at Trinity House and that Trinity House might have responsibilities for the surveillance and maintenance of pilot boats.

Other Issues (Chapter 11)

Provisional Licences

Rec 24 We *recommend* that pilotage authorities should be able to issue provisional licences to meet transient needs subject to strict limitations on their number and with the right of appeal.

Pilotage to the Berth

Rec 25 We *recommend* that pilotage jurisdiction should *cover berthing and dock movements* and that, in *due course, all dock pilotage should be within the control of the pilotage authority.*

River Thames

Rec 26 We *recommend* bringing all Thames pilotage under one control while safeguarding the position of existing Thames watermen and apprentices and maintaining the local knowledge and skills required.

Compensation

Rec 27 We *recommend* that legislative provision be made for compensation in the event of redundancy.

Penalties

Rec 28 We *recommend* that the penalties in the 1913 Act be brought up to date.

Surveying of Pilot Craft

Rec 29 Standards of pilot craft vary and we *recommend* that consideration should be given to responsibility for survey being taken either by the Department of Trade, the Central Board or Trinity House.

Appendix B

PILOTAGE AUTHORITIES IN THE UNITED KINGDOM

Pilotage district	Name of pilotage authority	No. of licensed pilots on 31.12.73	No. of pilotage certificates in force on 31.12.73
England and Wales			
Arundel*	The Littlehampton Harbour Board	3	—
Barry	Barry Pilotage Authority	10	3
Berwick	Berwick Harbour Commissioners	3	3
Blyth	Blyth Pilotage Authority	10	—
Boston and Spalding*	Boston and Spalding Pilotage Authority	7	—
Bristol*	City of Bristol Corporation	33	4
Cardiff	Cardiff Pilotage Authority	21	3
Gloucester*	Gloucester Pilotage Authority	12	—
Hartlepool	Hartlepool Pilotage Authority	13	—
Humber*	British Transport Docks Board		
(1) Humber		139	35
(2) Goole		29	—
(3) Trent		21	—
King's Lynn*	King's Lynn Conservancy Board	10	—
Lancaster	Lancaster Port Commissioners	1	—
Liverpool*	Mersey Docks and Harbour Company	176	234
London* ‡	Trinity House London	486	144
Trinity House Outport Districts* ‡	Trinity House London	233	229
Manchester	Manchester Ship Canal Company	80	12
Newport	Newport Pilotage Authority	20	—
Port Talbot	Port Talbot Pilotage Authority	4	—
Sunderland	Sunderland Pilotage Authority	13	—
Swansea	Swansea Pilotage Authority	15	14
Tees	Tees Pilotage Authority	54	—
Trinity House of Newcastle upon Tyne	Trinity House of Newcastle upon Tyne		
(1) Amble		2	—
(2) Craster		—	—
(3) Holy Island		2	—
(4) North Sunderland		1	—
(5) Seaham		4	—
(6) Whitby		3	—
Tyne	Tyne Pilotage Authority	59	—
Wisbech*	Wisbech Corporation	2	—

*Indicates pilotage compulsory in part or whole of district.
‡See following table.

Appendix C

Pilotage district	No. of licensed pilots on 31.12.73		No. of pilotage certificates in force on 31.12.73
	Permanent	Provisional	
London			
(1) Channel	113	—	
(2) Cinque Ports	88	—	
(3) North Channel	127	—	144
(4) River Thames	113	—	
(5) River Medway	37	—	
(6) Colchester and Maldon	7	—	
(7) River Stour	1	—	—
Aberdovey	1	—	—
Barrow	5	1	—
Beaumaris and Caernarvon	2	—	—
Bridgwater	—	2	—
Bridport	1	—	—
Brixham	1	1	8
Carlisle	2	2	—
Dartmouth	1	1	11
Dee	3	—	—
Exeter	2	—	—
Falmouth	5	2	—
Fleetwood	1	2	25
Fowey (including Par and Charlestown)	8	—	—
Holyhead	1	5	30
Ilfracombe	—	1	6
Ipswich	11	—	—
Isle of Wight			
(1) Inward Sea Pilots	31	—	
(2) Outward Sea Pilots	34	—	81
(3) Cowes	2	—	
(4) Portsmouth	3	—	
Lowestoft	2	—	—
Milford Haven	18	—	12
Neath	1	1	—
Newhaven	3	—	22
Orford Haven	—	1	—
Padstow	1	1	—
Penzance (including Newlyn)	3	—	3
Plymouth	7	—	2
Poole	6	—	5
Portmadoc	1	1	—
Preston	16	—	—
Rye	—	3	—
Scilly	1	1	3
Shoreham	7	—	—
St Ives	—	—	—
Taw and Torridge	4	—	—
Teignmouth	3	—	—
Watchet	1	1	—
Wells	1	1	—
Weymouth	1	1	13
Whitehaven and Maryport	3	—	—
Woodbridge	—	—	—
Yarmouth and Southwold	12	—	8

Appendix D

UNITED KINGDOM PILOTS' ASSOCIATION
(U.K.P.A.)

There was no independent organisation for pilots' protection until 1884 when the United Kingdom Pilots' Association was set up at a meeting held in the Atheneum at Bristol on 11th June, 1884. Delegates present represented 27 ports, whilst a further 17 ports applied for enrolment.

The first officers of the Association were: Commander George Cawley. President; Captain Bedford Pim, R.N., M.P., Q.C., Counsel; Captain Henry Langdon of Bristol, Secretary; Robert Fowler, M.P., the Lord Mayor of London (created Baronet 1885); Captain Tamlin of Swansea (Treasurer); S. R. Liversedge of Liverpool; Edward Edwards of Cardiff. Among the honorary members were Sir John Ruleston, M.P. (Devonport), Sir Seymour King, M.P. (Hull), Charles Bradlaugh, M. P. and Lord Claude Hamilton, M.P.

The first officers of the Association formed the nucleus of the Pilotage Lobby within the House of Commons, and they had the support of Admiral Mayne, Mr Parnell, Dr Fox and Dr Tanner who represented Irish constituencies.

Conferences were held in London (1885), Liverpool (1886), South Shields (1887), Bristol (1888), London (1889), Cork (1890), Swansea (1891), Glasgow (1892), Belfast (1893), Hull (1894), Cardiff (1895), Dover (1896), Bristol (1897), Caernarvon Castle (1898), Sunderland (1899), Liverpool (1900), Hull (1901), Plymouth (1902), Queenstown (1903), Deal (1904), Glasgow (1905), Swansea (1906), Barrow-in-Furness (1907), Gravesend (1908) and London (1909) when Commander George Cawley, the first President of the U.K.P.A., attended his last Conference. Although a sick man, in his Presidential Address he was able to report that Mr Churchill, President of the Board of Trade, had appointed a Special Committee to enquire into the many and varied matters concerning pilots and pilotage.

The energies devoted by the pilots to pilotage affairs and the decisions they then made at their Conferences under the Presidency of Commander Cawley, welded together a powerful organisation, fully competent to represent pilots at both local and national levels.

As the major national body of pilots in the U.K., the Association has been fortunate in having as Presidents well-known personalities. From 1925, the President of the U.K.P.A. was Lord Apsley, D.S.O., M.C., M.P. (Bristol Central) until he died on active service in the Western Desert in 1942. Among the Honorary Vice-Presidents who assisted Lord Apsley were Lord Strabolgi, Lord Gisborough, Lord Dulverton, Viscount Caldecote, Sir Irving Albery, M.P., Sir Gilbert Parker, Bart., Sir A. Shirley Benn, M.P., The Rt. Hon. Sir Thomas Inskip, K.C., M.P., Colonel John Ward, M.P., Lt.-Commander The Hon. J. M. Kenworthy, R.N., M.P., Lt. Col. Sir Gilbert Wills, Bart, Sir Alexander Richardson and Sir William Seager.

From 1946 to 1947, Admiral Lord Mountevans, K.C.B., D.S.O. was the President of the U.K.P.A. and in 1949 Captain Sir Peter MacDonald, K.B.E., M.P. (Isle of Wight) became the sixth President of the Association until his death in 1962.

From July, 1963 the Association's President was The Rt. Hon. James Callaghan, P.C., M.P. His many appointments as a Minister of the Crown and Prime Minister in no way prevented him from retaining his position as the seventh U.K.P.A. President until 24th June, 1976.

Appendix E

THE EUROPEAN MARITIME PILOTS' ASSOCIATION
(E.M.P.A.)

The EUROPEAN MARITIME PILOTS' ASSOCIATION was founded in Antwerp on 28th January, 1963 by pilots representing Belgium, France, Italy, Germany and the Netherlands, its objects being:—

(a) To collate and exchange information relating to the professional, financial, legal and social aspects of pilotage generally, with a view to promoting solidarity amongst pilots of the various European countries by establishing an effective understanding between them.

(b) To take any action which might be thought appropriate or desirable in the interests of maintaining or improving the status and conditions of employment of pilots, and in particular to seek representation at meetings, conventions or conferences where any matter relating to pilotage is being discussed.

It is laid down that no action shall be taken by the Association which might be calculated to interfere with the autonomy of freedom of action of any National Pilots' Organisation.

The Association consists of Pilots' Organisations from any European country and such persons as may be elected Honorary Members. The President, each Vice-President, the Treasurer and Secretary must be pilots and representatives of members. It is further stipulated in the Rules that the President and each Vice-President (of whom there are three) shall be of different nationality.

Each member-country is entitled to be represented at the Annual General Meeting by three delegates.

The first General Meeting of the Association was held in Hamburg on 22nd October, 1963 when mandatories of seven pilots' associations approved and signed the rules which were drawn up in the English language.

The founders of E.M.P.A. were nationals of the European Economic Community who were convinced that a united Europe was bound to emerge from the Common Market.

A Pilot Charter, dealing with the legal social and financial aspects of the pilot's profession was adopted at the A.G.M. at Stockholm in 1975.

In 1976 E.M.P.A. Delegates represented 13 different European countries.

Appendix F

INTERNATIONAL MARITIME PILOTS' ASSOCIATION
(I.M.P.A)

The International Association was founded in Kiel, West Germany, in June, 1970 and officially launched under the Honorary Presidency of The Rt. Hon. James Callaghan, Member of Parliament (U.K.) in Amsterdam, Netherlands, in May, 1971. In May, 1972 the Council of the Inter-Governmental Maritime Consultative Organisation (I.M.C.O.) concurred with the view expressed by their Maritime Safety Committee that I.M.P.A. could contribute usefully to the work of I.M.C.O. on such matters as safety of navigation and life saving, etc., and recommended that Consultative Status be granted. Final formal ratification by the Assembly of I.M.C.O. was made in November, 1973.

The aids of the International Association are:
(a) To provide machinery for consultation and exchange of information.
(b) To collate and disseminate relevant technical information.
(c) To make available advice and information to encourage the combined interests of Member Countries and the status of Pilots.
(d) To seek representation on International Governmental and non-Governmental Organisations.
(e) To take any action which might be deemed desirable or expedient in the interests of Pilots or for the benefit of the profession.

The International Association, which consists of thirty-two Pilots' Organisations from twenty-six Maritime States, is governed by decisions of the General Meetings held every two years, and an Executive Committee which meets annually. There is also an International Technical Committee.

All business and meetings are conducted in the English language.

A major element in the work of I.M.P.A. has been to actively progress the safety aspect of pilotage by submission of papers at meetings of I.M.C.O., by making available advice to the relevant committees of I.M.C.O. and generally to disseminate information to the only specialised Agency of the United Nationals concerned with maritime affairs.

I.M.P.A. has through its existing machinery for consultation and exchange of information, as well as by means of its Notices and International Coastline News, provided the basis for expanding its international functions.

General Meetings have been held in Amsterdam, Netherlands (1971); in Houston, Texas, U.S.A.(1973); and the next General Meeting will be held in Middlesborough (U.K.) in November, 1976.

The following publications are produced:
Pilot International
Coastline News
I.M.P.A. Notices
I.T.C. Notices.

Appendix G

Inter-Governmental Maritime Consultative Organisation

PILOT HOISTS

The I.M.C.O. Maritime Safety Committee at its 27th Session this year

(a) **approved** *the following Recommendations on Performance Standards for Mechanical Pilot Hoists (marked Annexe XI) and requested that it be submitted to the I.M.C.O. Assembly for adoption:*

(b) **adopted** *the following amendment to Regulation 17, Chapter V of the Convention concerning Pilot Ladders and Mechanical Pilot Hoists (marked Annexe XII) and requested that the amendment of the text be communicated to all concerned in accordance with the provisions of Article IX of the Convention.*

ANNEXE XI

RECOMMENDATION ON PERFORMANCE STANDARDS FOR MECHANICAL PILOT HOISTS

1. GENERAL
1.1 Mechanical pilot hoists and ancillary equipment should be of such design and construction as to ensure that the pilot can be embarked and disembarked in a safe manner. The hoist should be used solely for the embarkation and disembarkation of personnel.
1.2 The working load should be the sum of the weight of the ladder and falls in the fully lowered condition and the maximum number of persons which the hoist is designed to carry, the weight of each person being taken as 150 kgs.
1.3 Every pilot hoist should be of such construction that when operating under the defined working load each component should have an adequate factor of safety having regard to the material used, the method of construction and the nature of its duty.
1.4 In selecting the materials of construction, due regard should be paid to the conditions under which the hoist will be required to operate.
1.5 The pilot hoist should be located within the parallel body length of the ship and clear of all discharges.
1.6 The operator should be able to control the hoist when he is in a standing position and looking over the ship's side for observing the hoist, even in its lowest position.
1.7 The manufacturer of the pilot hoist should supply with each installation an approved maintenance manual, together with a maintenance log;
Each installation should be kept in good order and maintained in accordance with the instructions of the manual. All maintenance and repairs of the installation should be recorded in the log.

2. CONSTRUCTION
2.1 The hoist will generally consist of the following three main parts, but hoist of other equally efficient constructions may be considered:
   (a) a mechanical powered appliance together with means for a safe passage from the hoist to the deck and *vice versa;*
   (b) two separate falls;
   (c) a ladder consisting to two parts:
      (i) a rigid upper part for the transportation of the pilot upwards or downwards;
      (ii) a lower part consisting of a short length of pilot ladder, which enables the pilot to climb from the pilot launch to the upper part of the hoist and *vice versa.*

2.2 Mechanical powered appliance

(a) The source of power for the winches may be electrical, hydraulic or pneumatic. In the case of a pneumatic system an exclusive air supply should be provided with arrangements to control its quality. It may be necessary to give special consideration to the selection of the type of source of power for ships engaged in the carriage of flammable cargoes. All systems should be capable of efficient operation under the conditions of vibration, humidity and change of temperature likely to be experienced in the vessel in which they are installed.

(b) The design of the winch should include a brake or other equally effective arrangement, such as a properly constructed worm drive, which is capable of supporting the working load in the event of power failure.

(c) Efficient hand gear should be provided to lower or recover the pilot(s) at a reasonable speed in the event of power failure. The brake or other arrangement in paragraph (b) above should be capable of supporting the working load when the hand gear is in use.

(d) Crank handle(s) provided for manual operation should, when engaged, be interlocked so that the power supply is automatically cut off.

(e) Hoist should be fitted with safety devices to automatically cut off the power supply when the ladder comes against any stop to avoid overstressing the falls or other parts of the hoist. However, in the case of hoist operated by pneumatic power, if the maximum torque available from the air motor cannot result in overstressing of the falls or other parts of the hoist, the safety cut-out device may be omitted.

(f) All hoist controls should incorporate an emergency stop to cut off the power supply.

(g) The winch controls should be clearly and durably marked to indicate the action to "Hoist", "Stop" and "Lower". The movement of these controls should correspond with the movement of the hoist returning to the stop-position when released.

(h) Efficient arrangements should be provided to ensure that the falls wind evenly onto the winch-drums.

(i) Pilot hoists should be securely attached to the structure of the ship. Proper and strong attachment points should be provided for hoists of the portable type on each side of the ship. Attachment of the pilot hoist should not be solely by means of the ship's side rails.

(j) The winch should be capable of hoisting or lowering the pilot(s) at a speed of between 15 and 30 metres per minute.

(k) There should be safe means of access between the top of the hoist and the deck and *vice versa*; such access should be gained directly by a platform securely guarded by handrails.

(l) Any electrical appliance associated with the **ladder section** of the hoist should be operated at a voltage not exceeding 25 volts.

2.3 Falls

(a) Two separate wire rope falls should be used, made of flexible steel of adequate strength and resistant to corrosion in a salt-laden atmosphere.

(b) Wire ropes should be securely attached to the winch-drums and the ladder. These attachments should be capable of withstanding a proof load of not less than 2.2 times the load on such attachments. The falls should be maintained at a sufficient relative distance from one another.

(c) The wire rope falls should be of sufficient length to allow for all conditions of freeboard encountered in service and to retain at least three turns on the winch-drums with the hoist in its lowest position.

2.4 Ladder Section

The ladder section should comprise a rigid and a flexible part, complying with the following requirements:

(a) The rigid part should be not less than 2.50 metres (7¾ feet) in length and be equipped in such a way that the pilot can maintain a safe position whilst being hoisted or lowered. Such parts should be provided with:

   (i) a sufficient number of steps to provide a safe and easy access to and from the platform referred to in paragraph 2.2, sub-paragraph (k);

   (ii) suitable protection against extremes of temperature to provide safe handholds and fitted with non-skid steps;

   (iii) a spreader at the lower end of not less than 1.80 metres (5 feet 10 inches). The ends of the spreader should be provided with rollers of adequate size which should roll freely on the ship's side during the whole operation of embarking or disembarking;

   (iv) an effective guard ring, suitably padded, so positioned as to provide physical support for the pilot without hampering his movements;

   (v) adequate means for communication between the pilot and the operator and/or the responsible officer who supervises the embarkation or disembarkation of the pilot;

(vi) whenever possible an emergency stop switch within easy reach of the pilot by means of which he may cut off the power.

(b) Below the rigid part mentioned in paragraph (a) above, a section of pilot ladder comprising 8 steps should be provided, constructed in accordance with the following requirements:

    (i) The steps of the pilot ladder should be:

        (1) of hardwood, or other material of equivalent properties, made in one piece free of knots, having an efficient non-slip surface; the four lowest steps may be made of rubber of sufficient strength and stiffness or of other suitable material of equivalent characteristics;

        (2) not less than 480 millimetres (19 inches) long, 115 millimetres (4½ inches) wide, and 25 millimetres (1 inch) in depth, excluding any non-slip device;

        (3) equally spaced not less than 300 millimetres (12 inches) nor more than 380 millimetres (15 inches) apart and be secured in such a manner that they will remain horizontal.

    (ii) No pilot ladder should have more than two replacement steps which are secured in position by a method different from that used in the original construction of the ladder and any steps so secured should be replaced as soon as reasonably practicable by steps secured in position by the method used in the original construction of the ladder. When any replacement step is secured to the side ropes of the ladder by means of grooves in the sides of the step, such grooves should be in the longer sides of the step.

    (iii) The side ropes of the ladder should consist of two uncovered manilla ropes not less than 60 millimetres (2¼ inches) in circumference on each side. Each rope should be continuous with no joins below the top step.

(c) The steps of the flexible pilot ladder and those of the rigid ladder should be in the same vertical line, of the same width, spaced vertically equidistant and placed as close as practicable to the ship's side. The handholds of both parts of the ladder should be aligned as closely as possible.

2.5 Operational aspects

(a) Rigging and testing of the hoist and the embarkation and disembarkation of a pilot should be supervised by a responsible officer of the ship. Personnel engaged in rigging and operating the hoist should be instructed in the safe procedures to be adopted and the equipment should be tested prior to the embarkation or disembarkation of a pilot.

(b) Lighting should be provided at night such that the pilot hoist overside, its controls and the position where the pilot boards the ship should be adequately lit. A lifebuoy equipped with a self-igniting light should be kept at hand ready for use. A heaving line should be kept at hand ready for use if required.

(c) A pilot ladder complying with the provisions of Regulation 17, Chapter V, of the 1960 Safety Convention, should be rigged on deck adjacent to the hoist and available for immediate use.

(d) The position on the ship's side where the hoist will be lowered should be indicated as well as possible.

(e) An adequate protected stowage position should be provided for the portable hoist. In very cold weather to avoid the danger of ice formation, the portable hoist should not be rigged until use is imminent.

(f) The assembly and operation of the pilot hoist should form part of the ship's routine drills.

2.6 Testing

(a) Every new pilot hoist should be subjected to an overload test of 2.2 times the working load. During this test the load should be lowered a distance of not less than 5 metres (15 feet).

(b) An operating test of 10 per cent overload should be carried out after installation on board the ship to check the attachment and performance of the hoist to the satisfaction of the Administration.

(c) Subsequent examinations of the hoists under working conditions should be made at each survey for the renewal of the vessel's safety equipment certificate.

Appendix H

PROPOSED AMENDMENTS TO REGULATION 17, CHAPTER V OF THE 1960 SAFETY CONVENTION

The proposed text of Regulation 17, as amended, reads:

Regulation 17

Pilot ladders and mechanical pilot hoists

Ships engaged on voyages in the course of which pilots are likely to be employed shall comply with the following requirements:

(a) **Pilot ladders**

(i) The ladder shall be efficient for the purpose of enabling pilots to embark and disembark safely, kept clean and in good order and may be used by officials and other persons while a ship is arriving at or leaving port.

(ii) The ladder shall be secured in a position so that it is clear from any possible discharges from the ship, that each step rests firmly against the ship's side, that it is clear so far as is practicable of the finer lines of the ship and that the pilot can gain safe and convenient access to the ship after climbing not less than 1.5 metres (5 feet) and not more than 9 metres (30 feet). A single length of ladder shall be used capable of reaching the water from the point of access to the ship: in providing for this due allowance shall be made for all conditions of loading and trim of the ship and for an adverse list of 15°. Whenever the distance from sea level to the point of access to the ship is more than 9 metres (30 feet), access from the pilot ladder to the ship shall be by means of an accommodation ladder or other equally safe and convenient means.

(iii) The steps of the pilot ladder shall be:

(1) of hardwood, or other material of equivalent properties, made in one piece free of knots, having an efficient non-slip surface; the four lowest steps may be made of rubber of sufficient strength and stiffness or of other suitable material of equivalent characteristics;

(2) not less than 480 millimetres (19 inches) long, 115 millimetres (4½ inches) wide, and 25 millimetres (1 inch) in depth, excluding any non-slip device;

(3) equally spaced not less than 300 millimetres (12 inches) nor more than 380 millimetres (15 inches) apart and be secured in such a manner that they will remain horizontal.

(iv) No pilot ladder shall have more than two replacement steps which are secured in position by a method different from that used in the original construction of the ladder and any steps so secured shall be replaced as soon as reasonably practicable by steps secured in position by the method used in the original construction of the ladder. When any replacement step is secured to the side ropes of the ladder by means of grooves in the sides of the step, such grooves shall be in the longer sides of the step.

(v) The side ropes of the ladder shall consist of two uncovered manilla ropes not less than 60 millimetres (2¼ inches) in circumference on each side. Each rope shall be continuous with no joins below the top step. Two man-ropes properly secured to the ship and not less than 65 millimetres (2¼ inches) in circumference and a safety line shall be kept at hand ready for use if required.

(vi) Battens made of hardwood, or other material of equivalent properties, in one piece and not less than 1.80 metres (5 feet 10 inches) long shall be provided at such intervals as will prevent the pilot ladder from twisting. The lowest batten shall be on the fifth step from the bottom of the ladder and the interval between any batten and the next shall not exceed 9 steps.

(vii) Means shall be provided to ensure safe and convenient passage on to or into and off the ship between the head of the pilot ladder or of any accommodation ladder or other appliance provided. Where such passage is by means of a gateway in the rails or bulwark, adequate handholds shall be provided. Where such passage is by means of a bulwark ladder, such ladder shall be securely attached to the bulwark rail or platform and two handhold stanchions shall be fitted at the point of boarding or leaving the ship not less than 0.70 metre (2 feet 3 inches) nor more than 0.80 metre (2 feet 7 inches) apart. Each stanchion shall be rigidly secured to the ship's structure at or near its base and also at a higher point, shall be not less than 40 millimetres (1½ inches) in diameter and shall extend not less than 1.20 metres (3 feet 11 inches) above the top of the bulwark.

(viii) Lighting shall be provided at night such that both the pilot ladder overside and also the position where the pilot boards the ship shall be adequately lit. A lifebuoy equipped with a self-igniting light shall be kept at hand ready for use. A heaving line shall be kept at hand ready for use if required.

(ix) Means shall be provided to enable the pilot ladder to be used on either side of the ship.

(x) The rigging of the ladder and the embarkation and disembarkation of a pilot shall be supervised by a responsible officer of the ship.

(xi) Where on any ship constructional features such as rubbing bands would prevent the implementation of any of these provisions, special arrangements shall be made to the satisfaction of the Administration to ensure that persons are able to embark and disembark safely.

(b) **Mechanical pilot hoists**

(i) A mechanical pilot hoist, if provided, and its ancillary equipment shall be of a type approved by the Administration. It shall be of such design and construction as to ensure that the pilot can be embarked and disembarked in a safe manner including a safe access from the hoist to the deck and *vice versa*.

(ii) A pilot ladder complying with the provisions of paragraph (a) of this Regulation shall be kept on deck adjacent to the hoist and available for immediate use.

Pilot disembarking from ss *Hemiglypta*.   *A Shell Photograph*

Bibliography

A Report on Pilot Boarding Methods Overseas, Port Phillip Pilots, Melbourne, 1974
Cornish Shipwrecks, the South Coast, Richard Larn, David & Charles.
Discovering Ports and Harbours, Rowland W. Purton, University of London Press.
Harbour Pilotage, R. H. B. Ardley, Faber and Faber.
History of Pilotage and Navigational aids of the River Humber, 1512-1908, Arthur Storey, Trinity House of
    Kingston upon Hull.
History of the Liverpool Pilotage Service, John S. Rees.
On the Hooghly, M. H. Beattie, Philip Allan, 1935.
Pilot Aboard, John Radford, W. Blackwood, 1966.
Pilot Stations of the British Isles, arranged by John Radford, Brown Sons & Ferguson, Glasgow, 1939.
Pilot Take Charge, W. Bartlett Price, Brown Sons & Ferguson.
Port Phillip Pilots and Defences, Captain Noble, Hawthorn Press, Melbourne, 1974.
State Pilotage in America, a Report.
300 Years of Glorious Service, Pilots of the River Hooghly, 1669-1969.
To Minnie with Love, Jane Vansittart, Peter Davies, 1974/75.
Trinity House of Deptford, G. G. Harris, Athlone Press, London University.
Trinity House, Commander Hilary P. Mead, Sampson Low, Marston.
Trinity House of Kingston upon Hull, Arthur Storey, Trinity House of Kingston upon Hull, 1967.
Wreck and Rescue on the Essex Coast, Robert Malster, D. Bradford Barton, Truro, 1968.

Unfurling Trinity House flag aboard the *Pathfinder.*   *Barratt's*

Index

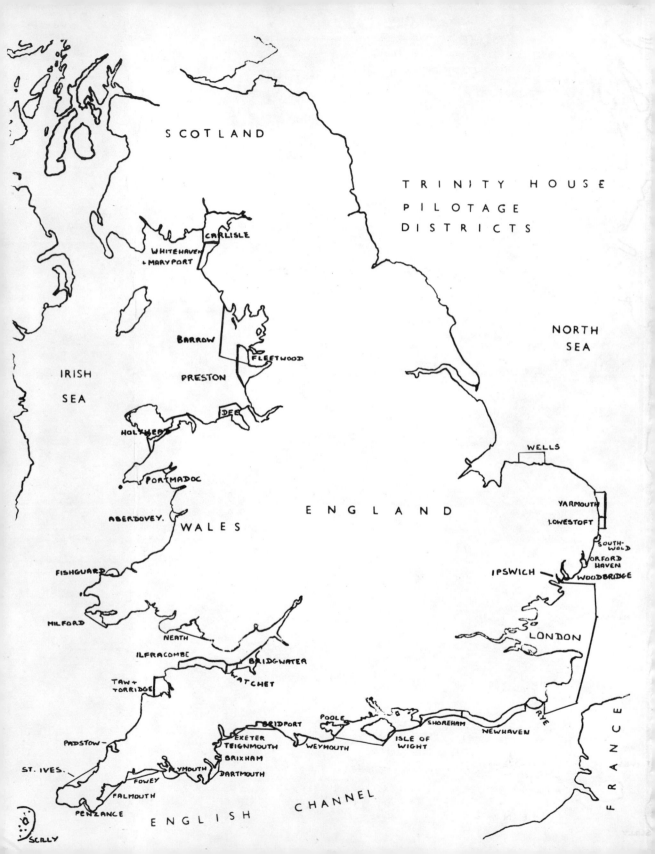